# McKim, Mead & White, Architects

Richard Guy Wilson

# M<sup>c</sup>KIM, MEAD & WHITE

*Architects*

RIZZOLI
NEW YORK

Published in the United States of America in 1983 by
RIZZOLI INTERNATIONAL PUBLICATIONS, INC.
712 Fifth Avenue, New York, NY 10019
Copyright © 1983 Richard Guy Wilson

Library of Congress Cataloging in Publication Data
Wilson, Richard Guy.
    McKim, Mead & White, architects.
    Bibliography: p.
    Includes index.
    1. McKim, Mead & White.    2. Architecture, Modern—
19th century—United States.    2. Architecture, Modern—
20th century—United States.    I. Title.    II. Title:
McKim, Mead, and White, architects.
NA737.M4W54    1983        720'.92'2        83-4534
ISBN 0-8478-0491-7

Designed by John Bradford

Set in type by Roberts/Churcher

Printed by the John D. Lucas Printing Company

to Ellie

# Acknowledgments

Over the years many individuals have contributed to my knowledge of the work of McKim, Mead & White. I would especially like to thank Leonard K. Eaton of the University of Michigan, who many years ago encouraged my pursuit of the trail of McKim, Mead & White. Wilson Duprey, former curator of the Map and Print Room at The New-York Historical Society, who provided help at early stages in my research. Sidney K. Robinson of Iowa State University has been constantly supportive. At different times research grants have been provided to me by the University of Michigan, Iowa State University and the University of Virginia. Many former and present colleagues and students have contributed ideas and insights too numerous to mention, yet of critical importance in a study such as this. I would also like to recognize the help of: Dianne Pilgrim of the Brooklyn Museum; Wendy Shadwell of The New-York Historical Society; Janet Davis of Baltimore; Ginette de B. Merrill of Belmont, Massachusetts; Lewis Sharp of the Metropolitan Museum of Art; Christopher Monkhouse of the Rhode Island School of Design; Ronald A. Chapin of the Delaware North Companies; Francis Kowsky of Buffalo State University; Leland M. Roth of the University of Oregon; Drexel Turner of Rice University; Sean Sculley of Simon Thoreson Associates; Susan Lemke of the National Defense University; Sue Kohler of the Fine Arts Commission, Washington, D.C.; Emily Hoxie of Peacedale, Rhode Island; Wallace Campbell of North Kingston, Rhode Island; Jay Sadler of Litchfield, Connecticut; William Voelke of the Pierpont Morgan Library; David Huntington of the University of Michigan; Nickolaus LeRoy King of Newport and New York; John Cherol of the Preservation Society of Newport County; Brendan Gill of New York; Ellen Molloy of the Trustees of Reservations; Allan Greenberg of New Haven; Joseph Disponzio of New York; William E. Barrett of Middleville, Virginia; John H. Dryfhout of the Saint-Gaudens National Site; and many others, whose kindness and help I needed. I especially want to thank my editor, Lynne Creighton-Neall; Marlene Heck of the Texas Historical Commission; and the owners of the many McKim, Mead & White buildings who opened their doors to me.

# Contents

# M^cKIM, MEAD & WHITE
## *Architects*

In contrast to the general air of misunderstanding that greeted the work of contemporaries such as Hector Guimard, Charles Rennie MacKintosh and Frank Lloyd Wright, critics and commentators never had any problem in understanding the intentions of McKim, Mead & White. Royal Cortissoz, writing about Pennsylvania Station, observed: "The march of those columns is superb, luring the eye until it forgets the immobility of walls, cornices and so on, and is lost in sensuous delight. It is a huge structure, and, for the mind sensitive to the great pageant of our material progress, it is fraught with ideas of tremendous and even ruthless power."[1] Sir Charles Reilly, head of the Liverpool School of Architecture, claimed in 1910 after viewing the New York works of McKim, Mead & White: "America has seized the lead, and . . . has established an architecture which, while satisfying the most exigent of modern requirements, is yet the conscious heir, as ours, let us hope, is in part the unconscious, of those forms and thoughts which, born in Greece more than 2,000 years ago, have been for the last four centuries, and must always be, with negligible deviations, the spring and motive of our life and art."[2]

Not that McKim, Mead & White ever hid their intentions. Charles McKim as early as 1877 called for the development of historical consciousness with regard to colonial buildings, or what he called "antiquarian architects—men who are familiar with the history of building, who are sufficiently versed in the principles of design to describe and note what-

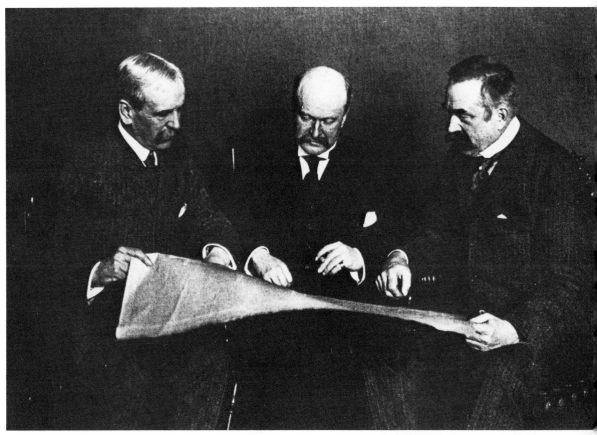

1. *William R. Mead, Charles F. McKim and Stanford White*

ever they may meet."[3] Later, after founding the American Academy in Rome, McKim claimed: "As Rome went to Greece, and later France, Spain and other countries had gone to Rome for their own reactions to the splendid standards of Classic and Renaissance Art, so must we become students, and delve, bring back and adapt to conditions here, a groundwork on which to build."[4]

The range of McKim, Mead & White's architecture was broad, from rambling informal country houses, such as the Alden house, to strident Imperial urban commissions, like the Girard Trust

9

2. *Pennsylvania Railroad Station,
Seventh Avenue facade,
New York, 1902–11*

of the principal designers, McKim and White, is about nine hundred.[5] The office name persisted until 1961, but with White's death in 1906, McKim's in 1909 and Mead's substantial withdrawal very shortly thereafter, analysis is confined to buildings designed before 1909, including, where appropriate, pre-partnership work.

**The Partners**  Contemporaries constantly stressed the different personalities of the three partners: McKim, the deliberate and persuasive scholar who aspired to the large and grand in both architecture and ideas; Mead, the quiet, unoriginal designer involved in the intricate details of running an office; and Stanford White, the mercurial firebrand of energy and motion, a specialist in the quick effect. The differences might be said to make up an ideal architectural partnership, with the similarities hardly noticed. All three men came from the class of the intellectual elite of the pre-Civil War years. Their families were educated though not particularly wealthy. They grew up in the ideals and ferment of the 1850s, saw those same ideals dashed in the sixties, and then replaced in the seventies, eighties and nineties with a new ethic of wealth and nationalism.

Charles Follen McKim (1847–1909) was born in Pennsylvania, the son of a professional, radical, abolitionist father and a Quaker mother. He spent 1866–67 at Harvard studying engineering, a summer in the office of the Ruskin infatuated Russell Sturgis, and then 1867–70 at the Ecole des Beaux-Arts in the atelier of Daumet. In 1870, he returned

Company. These reflect changing concerns of function, formal aesthetics, relationship to history and appropriate images for Americans. My intent in this essay is to briefly outline the partners' lives and personalities, and in more depth explore their office methods, their architectural development, their City Beautiful design, their process of eclecticism and design and ultimately the meaning of their architecture. A concluding section provides an in-depth study of thirty-one examples of their work—some of the buildings are well known, others have never been published.

A note here on coverage of works is in order. The total number of buildings and projects completed during the lives

3. Mrs. A. C. Alden house,
Lloyd's Neck, Long Island, 1879.
Designed by McKim, Mead & Bigelow.

to the United States and entered the New York office of H. H. Richardson, where he worked on the Brattle Street Church and the competition drawings for Trinity Church. He began to separate from Richardson in 1872 and informally associated with William Mead until 1877, when a formal partnership was created. The partnership of 1877 also included William Bigelow, a brother-in-law of McKim's (McKim married Annie Bigelow in 1874). Bigelow left the firm in 1879 after McKim's divorce, and Stanford White entered as a junior partner in September 1879. In 1885, McKim married Julia Appleton, a member of a wealthy Boston family; she died barely a year later. An extremely social man, McKim tended to devote his later life to more public causes, such as the World's Columbian Exposition, the American School of Architecture in Rome (later the American Academy in Rome), the Washington, D.C., Plan of 1901–02 and the American Institute of Architects. Frequent trips to England, the Continent, and the Near East in the company of artist friends and wealthy clients kept him well-supplied with ideas and images.

As the only partner to commit ideas to paper, McKim was the leading member and spokesman for the firm. He was responsible for some of the larger commissions: the Boston Public Library, Pennsylvania Station, Columbia University and the Morgan Library. His designs tended toward the monumental and academic, reflecting both his somewhat pompous personality and his education. McKim had a learned bookish quality and employees recalled his

4. Girard Trust Company, Philadelphia, 1904–09.
The initial plans were done by McKim
and, after his death, were completed by
William Symmes Richardson.

searching through Letarouilly's *Edifices de Rome Moderne* or other tomes for the correct motive or detail. His office nickname was Bramante. Trained in an architectural system that put a premium on memory of *partis,* orders and details, he could design aloud, or as one draughtsman recalled: "He liked to sit down at a draftsman's table, usually in his hat and immaculate shirt sleeves, and design out loud . . . the room reverberated with architectural terms . . . Cyma Recta; Cyma Reversa; Fillet above; Fillet below; Dentils; Modillions: and so on."[6]

William Rutherford Mead (1846–1928) was born in Brattleboro, Vermont. His father was a lawyer and his mother came from the radically inclined

11

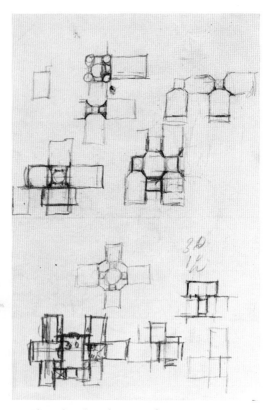

5. *Floor plans by White, pencil on paper*

Noyes family. A brother, Larkin, would become a well-known sculptor, and a sister, Elinor, was a painter who would marry William Dean Howells. After graduation from Amherst College in 1867 he apprenticed with an engineer and spent two years in the Russell Sturgis office (after McKim's departure). In 1871, Mead made the obligatory European pilgrimage and studied informally at the Accademia delle Belle Arti in Florence. His life, after joining up with McKim and then White, appears to have been uneventful. He married in 1884; he took part in the high life of artists and clubs in New York and made the usual European visits. Mead's office position was the adjudicator or, as he remarked, to keep his partners from "making damn fools of themselves." A few plans, such as the Rhode Island State House, came from his pen, but his major contribution was to run the office and to be critic of his partners' ideas. Stanford White's son, later a partner in the firm, noted: "*Vogue la Galere* was the motto of the firm; and if McKim was the hull and White the sails of the ship, Mead was both rudder and anchor."[7] His office nickname was "Dummy," reflecting not his intelligence but his quiet, noncommittal New England demeanor.

Stanford White (1853–1906) was born in New York City, the son of an impoverished literary and music critic. His father craved recognition and monetary reward, and, as an extreme Anglophile, especially with regard to English country houses, undoubtedly influenced his son. An early talent for sketching and watercolors led White to consider study-ing painting with John La Farge. Perceiving the lack of financial reward as a painter, White entered the office of H. H. Richardson in 1872 as an apprentice, just as McKim was beginning to separate from the office. White spent 1872–78 there, becoming the ornamental and decorative expert, and perfecting his quick and impressionistic rendering style. Never very interested in domestic house design, Richardson treated White as a coequal on projects such as the Watts Sherman house. In 1878, feeling his lack of any European experience, White left Richardson and traveled for over a year on the Continent before returning in September 1879, and taking Bigelow's place in the New York office of McKim and Mead.

Like McKim, White's personal life and professional career became inseparable. He married Bessie Smith of Long Island in 1884 and took a six-month honeymoon of Europe and the Near East, sightseeing and purchasing antiquities for his own and clients' collections. Back in New York he became well-known with his loud clothes, red hair and moustache and ebullient personality. He traversed the world of the artist, many of whom were his close friends, and high society, for whom he produced houses and party decorations. The attractions of money and flesh were irresistible, and he found himself caught in an orbit of increasingly frenzied demand. In June 1906, an earlier affair with model Evelyn Nesbit resulted in White's murder by her new husband on the roof garden of Madison Square Garden, a building designed by White some sixteen years

*Rhode Island State House*

*McMillan Plan, Washington, D.C.*

*Edgar House*

earlier. The ensuing trial became a *cause célèbre* of the yellow press and scandalmongers, leaving White with a reputation as a notorious playboy.

White's office nickname "Benvenuto Cellini" reveals his position towards design as essentially a matter of ornament and elaboration of motifs. While White stayed longer with Richardson than did McKim, he seemed to have been less affected; his personal style never attained the solidity and consolidation that united McKim and Richardson. It may be the common Beaux-Arts background that directed both McKim and Richardson towards an architecture of weight and gravity. White, on the contrary, remained tied to a pictorial vision of architecture, dazzling surface effects of light, texture, color and ornament. A brilliant ornamentalist, he turned his hand to almost any project: interiors, furniture, jewelry, picture frames, book and magazine covers, and bases for statues by friends such as Augustus Saint-Gaudens and Frederick MacMonnies. Interiors were perhaps his greatest architectural accomplishment, for intuitively he disregarded the commonly accepted rules. More than rich, but gaudy and sensuous, White created his own unique brand of interior decoration, mixing styles, periods, textures and colors. He imported large quantities of *objets d'art* from fragments of buildings to entire rooms and sold them to clients. The frenetic quality of his interiors gives a clue to his working methods, and in contrast to the caution and care of McKim and Mead, he would scrawl out designs, or as an office member recalled:

"He would tear into your alcove, perhaps push you off your stool with his body while he reached for pencil and tracing paper and in five minutes make a dozen sketches of some arrangement of detail or plan, slam his hand down on one of them—or perhaps two or three of them if they were close together—say 'Do that', and tear off again. You had to guess what and which he meant."[8] Exasperating to work with, White could often be difficult, as a letter from a client noted, "I must ask you to dictate an immediate reply—and see that it gets mailed." "White," J. P. Morgan claimed, "is always crazy."[9]

6. *Colonel Robert Gould Shaw Memorial, Boston, Massachusetts, 1884–97*

7. *Office of McKim, Mead & White,*
*1 West 20 Street, New York, ca. 1891*

of an atelier where "art" was uppermost, or, as White once wrote: "The architects who have made their mark in the world are artists and designers of buildings, and not engineers and businessmen."[11] In fact, a system did exist. Specification writing, presentation drawings, construction supervision, preliminary design and working drawings were all carried out by those in the office who specialized within each discipline. During the first twelve years of the office's existence (1879–91), close collaboration between the partners and employees existed. As the firm grew increasingly large, however, the office began to change, both physically and in the scale of work. First, the firm moved into larger quarters which tended to isolate the partners from the drafting room and each other. Consequently, the interaction between the partners on design matters tended to diminish, and projects increasingly betrayed the hand of a single designer rather than all three. Additionally, beginning in the late 1880s, a change in project scale occurred as the smaller resort and country cottages disappeared from the office and larger commissions were sought, such as Columbia University and very large country estates. This change in scale and number of projects meant that the quantity of time each partner could spend on a project diminished, and the role of the draughtsmen increased. Inevitably, some designs betrayed a certain blandness, and an impersonal office style appeared with some buildings. Still the firm claimed a true collaboration existed. In 1886, Stanford White admonished an art magazine: "No

**Office Methods** The New York office where most of the work was produced (for brief periods there were branch offices in Boston and Kansas City) varied in size depending on the volume of work. In the early 1880s it numbered ten to twelve, but in the early 1890s and again in the 1900s, after a severe depression in the mid-1890s, the office numbered well over one hundred.[10]

In spite of size, the partners liked to claim they were not a "plan factory," rather they ran the office along the lines member of our firm is ever individually responsible for any design which goes out from it," and later in 1902, McKim requested President Theodore Roosevelt to use the firm's name and not his, personally, when discussing the new War College.[12]

Within such a large and complex office, the draughtsman and/or assistant assumed a large role, either in developing one of the partners' primary schemes, or in some cases becoming the sole author of a design. Shortly before White's murder in 1906, the partnership had been expanded to include William Mitchell Kendall, who had been with the firm since 1882, Bert L. Fenner, who entered in 1891 and William Symmes Richardson, who had joined in 1895. Each of these men had been assistants to a partner (Kendall for McKim, Fenner for Mead and Richardson for White) and had taken major responsibility for designs—such as Columbia University (Kendall) and Pennsylvania Station (Richardson). The atelier quality was true in the sense that a large number of architects received encouragement and training in the McKim, Mead & White offices before they went on to their own practices. These men included Cass Gilbert, Henry Bacon, John Galen Howard, H. Van Buren Magonigle, Frank Hoppin, John Merven Carrère, Thomas Hastings, Austin Lord, Edward Palmer York, Philip Sawyer and many other men in New York and regional firms across the United States. Cass Gilbert was with the McKim, Mead & White office for nearly two years in the early 1880s, and after returning to St. Paul,

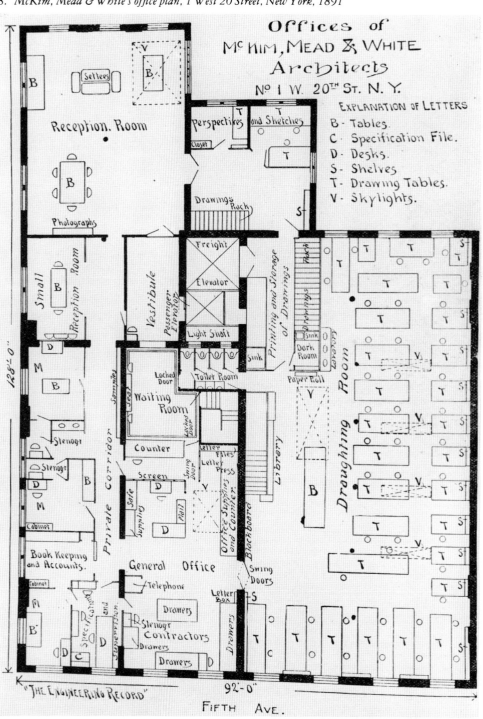

9. Henry G. Villard houses,
New York, 1882–86

10. Ross Winans house,
Baltimore, Maryland.
Fountain design
by Cass Gilbert, 1882.

Minnesota, maintained close relations with the New York office and collaborated on several projects. Gilbert's knowledge of the personal hand of the principal designers is testified to by a fountain in the Winans house in Baltimore. The low relief dolphines and detail is distinctly reminiscent of White's and Saint-Gauden's work on the base of Farragut Monument. Gilbert, who supervised construction in Baltimore, designed the entire fountain himself.

Illustrative of the complexities of assigning credit is the myth of Joseph Morrill Wells and the design of the Villard houses. Wells (1853–90) was born in Boston and trained with several architects before joining the McKim and Mead office shortly before White. His celebration of the Renaissance and classic styles over the Gothic became legendary, and combined with a cynical wit and malicious tongue he could reduce a design to shreds. Large drawings of the Louvre and Farnese palaces became his trademark. Wells's actual role in the office is debatable; later defenders of the office such as Kendall claimed Wells was principally responsible for details. However, the overall "ensemble," Kendall claimed, was always by one of the partners.[13] Yet Kendall did admit Wells's "stand for the classic and particularly the Italian style of architecture," had an important influence on the firm. Certainly the partners had a healthy respect for his talents and evidently tendered him a partnership; he declined with the reply he would not "put his name to so much damned bad work."[14] The Russell and Erwin Building in New Britain, Connec-

ticut, an early example of Italian Renaissance precedent, is generally credited solely to Wells.

The design for the Villard houses was more complex. The commission, by Henry Villard, a wealthy railroad promoter—for a large city house for himself and for five smaller houses on a lot in midtown Manhattan—came through McKim, who was distantly related to Villard by marriage. The actual sequence of events is unclear, but evidently McKim, Mead and Villard worked out a scheme for the six houses grouped around a courtyard and turned the facade design over to White, who did a quick study in a sort of Richardson Romanesque-Queen Anne style (similar to the Tiffany houses) and then left town. Wells assumed the project and redesigned the exterior following the precedent of the Cancelleria in Rome. Writing to Cass Gilbert a few years later, after the facade was completed, Wells complained: "I hope that eventually these works will be ascribed to their actual authors—as I do not think that either White nor McKim care a damn about it."[15] The exterior of the houses marked a shift in the firm's work towards a more monumental scale and the usage of identifiable Italian Renaissance sources. Wells's redesign of the exterior certainly received the partners' approval, for unilaterally he would never have made that decision. Many designers contributed to the final result: Stanford White designed the staircase, hall and dining room and George Fletcher Babb was responsible for the drawing room. Babb would soon leave McKim, Mead & White to form his own firm,

*12. John Howard Whittemore house, Middlebury, Connecticut, 1894–96*

**Architectural Development** From the vast output of McKim, Mead & White, ranging from the early individual essays of the 1870s to the works of the 1900s, a bewildering variety of forms, styles, motifs and images loom up with little apparent system or order. In actuality, however, the styles and images do represent a rational eclecticism connected either with historical association, the enterprise involved, or because a principle of architectural order was felt necessary. Beyond the eclecticism and meaning of style (which will be treated later) a pattern of development emerges concerned with shifts in emphasis of form, outline, material, space and ornament, a development that parallels the growth of classicism in the firm's work.

Almost any comparison of early and later buildings will reveal a greater degree of apparent symmetry, facade organization and repeated geometric forms with the later designs. Even when essentially ahistorical idioms were used in later buildings, such as the shingled Howard Whittemore house, the reliance upon a symmetrical organization is evident. The different usage of historical precedent is observable in a comparison of two houses: one earlier, the Metcalfe of 1882–84, and one later, the Oerlichs of 1897–1902. The Oerlichs house design was indebted to the Grand Trianon for the ground-floor motifs; however, Stanford White, who was the principal designer, did not adopt the spreading scheme of the Grand Trianon, but rather the house was self-contained and free-standing. He also added a second floor. In the Metcalfe house no such specific

Babb, Cook & Willard, and in 1886 he would be hired to make some exterior alterations to the houses. All the major partners, as well as several employees, were involved in essential aspects of the design of the Villard houses, and, as in all large architectural offices, collaboration was the key.

source is observable, and while its style was known as "conventionalized 'early colonial,'" the designer—probably White—drew on no known prototype.[16] With later buildings the specific source is sometimes more observable, but never is there a wholesale copying of an entire building.

The "figure in the carpet" is a drive towards clarity, control and order. Within this overall movement towards order, three stages emerge, overlapping and yet roughly chronological: an "Early Period" from the 1870s through the mid-1880s; a "Consolidation Period," from the early 1880s through the early 1890s; and a "High Classical Period," from the late 1880s through 1909.

In McKim, Mead & White's work of the Early Period there is a tendency towards lightness of form; walls, whether of shingles or brick, appear as thin coverings stretched around the irregular volumes of interior spaces. Exterior massing is largely determined by the interior space arrangement. Plan organization is functional, with major spaces grouped around a central hall containing vertical circulation. Symmetry, when it appears, is largely a by-product of the organization, and not a conscious gesture. Much has been written about the "open" plan of resort houses, such as the Bell house, whose sliding doors could be pushed back to interconnect the public rooms.[17] In such houses though, each room was treated as a particularized space with its own function and decor. There is a tendency towards consolidation and regularization that frequently takes the form of a prominent, encom-

passing roof, as in the Howells house or the Newport Casino. The creation of a varying module, as in the bays of the Moses Taylor house, allowed McKim to impart a sense of order to an inherently disordered scheme. Still a variety of wall surface, color, texture and stylistic references dominates.

Stylistic references are wide ranging in the Early Period and include Queen Anne in the Casino and the Tilton house, Francois I$^{er}$ in the Winans house, Japanese in the Kingscote's dining room and North German vernacular in the

13. "Rosecliff," Herman and Tessie Oerlichs house, Newport, Rhode Island, 1897–1902

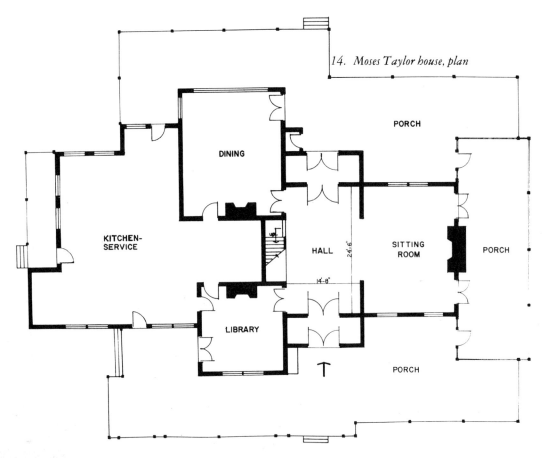

14. *Moses Taylor house, plan*

DINING

PORCH

KITCHEN-SERVICE

HALL

SITTING ROOM

PORCH

LIBRARY

PORCH

24'-6"

14'-8"

15. *Moses Taylor house, Elberon, New Jersey, 1876–77. Designed by McKim before joining Mead and Bigelow, it is a early example of the "modernized Colonial" style.*

Tiffany house. A fascination with the exotic Near East can be seen in many of the screens of spindels from the period. Details from American seventeenth and eighteenth centuries, such as shingles, pediments, elliptical windows and broad sloping roofs, caused many of the houses such as the Bell house to be called "modernized colonial."[18] The Ward house in Lenox with its simulated appearance of growth over time made one commentator claim "that but for a few Queen Anne Fantasies it might pass for an old Puritan's homestead."[19]

During the second period, a time of consolidation from the early 1880s to early 1890s, the freedom of form and lightness was replaced by more regular geometrical forms and solidarity. The physical weight and density of the Villard group indicated this direction, and Wells claimed they were the only United States buildings "which [have] any scale or largeness."[20] In country houses, the lighter shingled idiom gave way to a heavier, more baronial idiom, as in the Osborn house. Parallel to the growth of a physical weight and size, there was also a gradual lightening of coloration. The Villard houses were built out of New York brownstone, though the firm had tried unsuccessfully to have Villard use a lighter-colored stone. By the late 1880s, as in the Boston Public Library, light-colored stone had become more prominent. Madison Square Garden and Judson Memorial Church, both designed by White, were highly colored, but the harsh polychrome of the High Victorian Gothic had dissipated.

Historical references in the Consolida-

16. *"Kingscote," David H. King, Jr., house,
Newport, Rhode Island, 1880–81*

17. *Samuel Gray Ward house, Lenox, Massachusetts, 1877–78. Designed by McKim in partnership with Mead and Bigelow.*

18. *Charles J. Osborn house, Mamaroneck, New York, 1883–85*

19. *H. A. C. Taylor house, Newport, Rhode Island, 1883–86*

tion Period became more obvious, whether it was the baronial, of "the border of the Loire or among the hills of England,"[21] as in the Osborn house; Georgian, as in the H.A.C. Taylor house; or Italian Renaissance, as in the Villard houses. They were not exact copies of any prototype, since no eighteenth-century American Georgian house had six Venetian windows, a short segment of Adamesque frieze and a range of porticos, as did the Taylor house. The Villard houses quoted the Cancelleria via Letarouilly, yet they were simplified in detail, lacking the upper-floor pilasters and entablature. Reversal of window pediments on the upper floor indicated a revised interior arrangement lacking a true *piano nobile*. The reversal also allowed an upward progression from simplicity to ornateness.

Implicit in the more historicizing work of the Consolidation Period was a greater degree of geometrical order in elevation and plan. Plans were more clearly organized, the path into and through a house was readily apparent and the ambiguity between front and entrance, as in the Bell house, disappeared. The irregularity of plans that represented an older picturesque idea of composition was gradually replaced with a new notion of order that implied a predetermined system of spatial regularity, axial entry, alignment of spaces and symmetry. A tensional conflict became evident, for example in the Boston Public Library, where the preestablished grand spaces conflicted with the reality of many smaller spaces. The Villard houses, coming as they did at the beginning of the Consoli-

20. *Morgan house from across inlet at Fort Adams*

21. *Morgan house, plan*

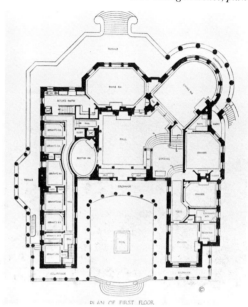

PLAN OF FIRST FLOOR

dation Period, exhibited a conflict between the geometrical organization of the facade and the plans—halls and rooms were frequently entered from the side or off center, and several entrances were tucked away to the rear.

The Low house, considered by some critics to be the culmination of the shingled expression, illustrates the tension between exterior and interior; the huge gable submerges all the usual outward-flung elements into a complete classical whole. McKim, the chief designer, allowed the dining and sitting rooms to push outward, breaking the straight-cut shingle skin, while the piazza creates a void at one end. On the interior, the compression is so strong that six different levels are necessary to fit it under the hugh gable.

The E. D. Morgan house is a clear example of the tensional balance between outward form and plan. Sited upon a rock outcropping, it is approached across a long causeway with twin, temple-front wings pushing forward to create a courtyard to greet the visitor. Entrance is straight upon axis, but upon entering the axis bends on the diagonal and pushes through the hall and out through the living room to create a huge swelling bay, overlooking the harbor. The prim and proper Ionic order that greets the visitor on the sophisticated Palladian

22. *"Beacon Rock," E. D. Morgan house, Newport, Rhode Island, 1889–91*

front becomes transformed into primitive random ashlar Doric columns on the harbor side. A resolution of the conflict between form and plan, or more specifically between the idea of a pre-existing order and the disharmonious functions to be housed, would only be possible with the dominance of one or the other. For McKim, Mead & White, the solution would be the reinterpreted laws of classicism.

In their work of the High Classical Period (late 1880s–1909), the drive toward preestablished order becomes more evident along with the even more literal quotations of historical reference. Elevations and plans are more compact and the individual functional differences of spaces are no longer allowed to disrupt the ideal order. The intermediate floors of bedrooms, and service areas in the University Club in New York are given a regular exterior appearance and appear as part of the tripartite elevation. Picturesqueness in general is calmed down, as is polychrome. Differences in color abound, but it is lighter colors—pinks, whites, creams, tans, yellows—that in general replace the earlier, deeper and more earthy browns, ochers, greens and reds. The Madison Square Presbyterian Church, one of White's last projects, consisted of a yellow-brick facade, trimmed in blue, green and yellow terra cotta, with Corinthian columns of polished-green granite, pediment figures in Della Robbia blues, a dome of green and yellow tiles and a gold finial.

The dominance of a preestablished order is particularly evident in the composition by McKim for Columbia University. The site, on rather high uneven ground in upper Manhattan, was altered into two platform levels on which a symmetrical grouping of buildings was placed. The plan was not of quadrangles, but rather buildings surrounding courtyards that culminated with terraces, balustrades and urns and the Low Library. No discernible module was used, or, if so, it was a varying one of ten to fifteen feet (the intercolumniation in the library measures approximately ten feet).

The original plan (modified in 1903 to include a south campus and side entry) made the Low Library the axis of the dominant approach. Clad in white limestone, the form of the library is a Greek cross with a shallow rising saucer dome. McKim, in a typical mood of historical justification, claimed this was from Roman *thermae* which, in addition to serving as "baths, were . . . Academies [and] . . . Public Libraries."[22] A giant order of Ionic columns serves as the portico and, from the terrace steps, the visitor's vision is engulfed by the monumental colonnade. Past the portico a cubical vestibule with a screen of columns gives access to the ambulatory and the brilliantly lighted central space. The functions of the library are completely secondary to the architectural and ritualistic nature. The central space with its four large, coffered arches, the beveled corner piers, the low saucer dome, the green verte marble columns and balconies with statues above, is clearly its own *raison d'être*. Thin wooden bookcases, reading tables and chairs had a quality of impermanence, while specialized libraries and administration were stuffed into

24. *"Harbour Hill," Clarence H. Mackay house, Roslyn, Long Island, 1899–1902*

the wings and stacks in the basement. In contrast to the Low Library, the other campus buildings are more frankly utilitarian in character, brick with limestone trim. Not too surprisingly, the building's use was discontinued as a library in 1934, and now serves as a ritualistic center for administration and displays.

Not all buildings of the High Classical Period would display such thorough commitment to an ideal of plan and form. Fittingly, country houses by Stanford White frequently have an appearance of order, but contain functional qualities of accommodation as well. The Oerlichs house, in spite of the apparent outer symmetry, used one wing as an entry sequence, in contrast to the other containing the dining room, billiard room and service areas. "Harbor Hill," the large country house for Clarence Mackay, had an austere outer symmetry, approach and entry, undercut by a subtlety that provided a prelude for the interior. The main approach road swung up a hill through fields and trees before turning and approaching dead on axis. Fifty feet before the entrance the road split to create a grassy oval, rejoining at the entrance terrace. This conflict in forward movement was mirrored on the interior where a strong cross-axial layering of space impeded forward movement; first the entrance hall, stair hall and billiard room slot; then in the center of the main hall the huge fireplace and doorway in the opposite wall created a second cross axis; and finally the far screen of columns indicated a third layer of the stone room and dining room. A substantial view was available from the rear, but of more importance was the formal garden which could only be seen on the cross axis of the salon. Again, White manipulated the view by placing a wall directly opposite the doorway, so only diagonal views of the piazza columns were possible. By moving completely off the axis and penetrating the outer wall of the salon could the cascade of the formal gardens be seen. A similar interior contradiction greets the visitor at "Florham," the Twombly house where the approach and facade belie the major cross-axial hall and staircase.

The formal development of McKim, Mead & White's architecture that has been sketched through the device of these three periods can be translated into the broader spectrum of late-nineteenth-century architecture. Historians have seen a general subsidence of picturesqueness around the turn of the century.[23] Instead of the highly agitated pyrotechnic displays of the years 1850 to 1880, turn-of-the-century architecture exhibited a tendency towards the horizontal. Towers and varied skylines certainly remained, as in McKim, Mead

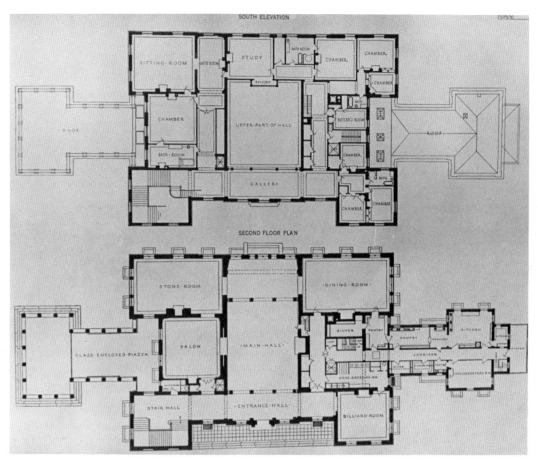

25. *Mackay house, plan*

26. *Mackay house, garden plan*

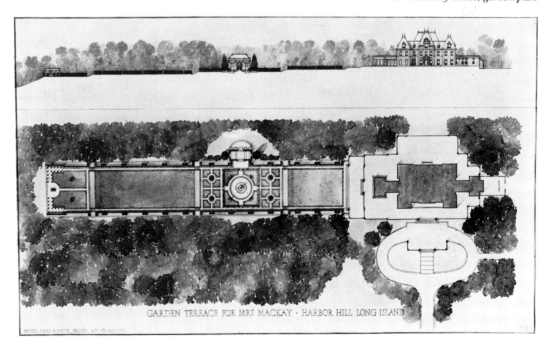

27. *New Haven and Hartford Railroad Station, Waterbury, Connecticut, 1906–09.*
*White began the design and, after his death, it was completed by William Symmes Richardson.*

& White's Waterbury Connecticut Railroad Station (1906–09), but even there, with the giant campaneli, the smoothness of the silhouette contrasted with mid-century variation. Parts—whether towers, turrets, wings, roofs, or ornaments, which had dominated buildings of the 1850s and 1880s—subsided back into the mass of the building. The mass reasserted itself and parts became fewer in number and larger in subdivision.

A striking indication of this reassertion of mass and subordination of parts can be seen in an office rendering for the Boston Public Library and Copley Square. The bird's-eye perspective of the preliminary plan for the library (before the triple-arched entrance had been decided upon) with its pink Milford granite exterior and solid, blocky horizontal form contrasts with the agitated brown decades of the 1870s that surround it. The library is an island of calm against the random forms and vertical accents of the Museum of Fine Arts, the New Old South Church, the S. S. Pierce store and Trinity Church. Against the energetic leaps of Richardson's Trinity, McKim's library stands as a pure classical form, stopping the dark aged aggressor.

**The City Beautiful**    McKim, Mead & White are generally acknowledged as the leading proponents of the specifically American response to the city, the so-called civic art or City Beautiful movement. They were responsible for the design of all types of urban elements: lamp standards, statue pedestals, park pavilions, triumphal arches, city houses, banks, office buildings and building complexes. The background of the City Beautiful movement can be traced as far back as the 1850s and the beginning of interest in urban parks. Not until the later 1880s did Americans begin to think of beautifying cities along classic lines. In 1888 Edward Bellamy published the immensely popular utopian novel, *Looking Backward, 2000–1887,* and prophesied the vision of "miles of broad streets, shaded by trees and lined with fine buildings, . . . large open squares filled with trees, among which statues glistened and fountains flashed . . . [and] public buildings of a colossal size and an architectural grandeur unparalleled."[24] Contemporary with Bellamy, McKim & White presented their prototype of civic art, the Boston Public Library (1887–95). The library offered in miniature a model for the city, for the interior was a series of public spaces, each with its own grand character and decoration. Turned inside out, the library could be the city. This treatment of the city as a series of particulated spaces, linked and yet each different, would dominate the early City Beautiful movement from the 1880s until the early 1900s. Beginning in 1901 the focus of the City Beautiful movement enlarged, and emphasis was placed

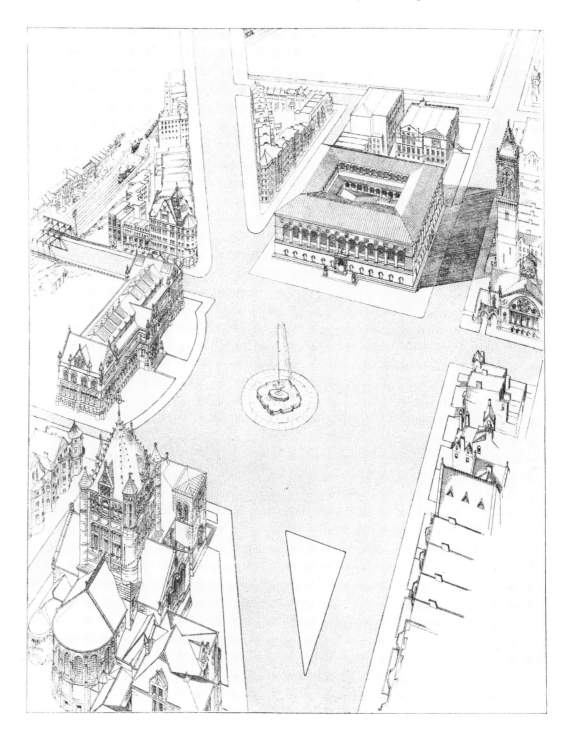

on redesigning larger areas of the city. Yet the underlying design approach of contrast was remarkably similar to the earlier more piecemeal treatment. In this treatment, really a form of an urban picturesque, McKim, Mead & White and their contemporaries were profoundly influenced by their suburban and country work. There were certainly obvious differences in strategies applied to the different situations, yet the way they treated the city must be considered as an urban picturesque vision.

Where McKim, Mead & White placed formal ensembles within the city, contrast was always apparent. For Columbia University and New York University they created acropolises located at high points overlooking the city. They were to be seen against the surrounding context of disunity which made them stand apart. In the McMillan Plan for Washington, D.C. (1901–02), on which McKim worked along with Daniel Burnham, Augustus Saint-Gaudens and Frederick Law Olmsted, Jr., the city was viewed as a composition of variety which needed focal points such as squares, parks and malls. Against the backdrop of disunity, the formal elements and the monumental structures would stand out: triumphal arches, plazas, gardens, watergates and ritualistic centers. To create the plan the McMillan Commission studied American as well as European precedent, traveling down the James River to see Georgian mansions, gardens along with the town of Williamsburg, and visited Europe to study the Place de la Concord in Paris and the gardens of the Vaux-le-Vicomte. Gardens and the insertion of greenery into Washington, and the American city in general, became one of the key elements in the American City Beautiful movement. In Washington, the commission recommended the removal of the surface railroad from the foot of the Capitol, the destruction of the old Smithsonian castle, the extensions of the cross axis at the Washington Monument, and the erection of a number of seemingly similar bland classical structures. However, it was never the goal for the rest of the city to be completely classicized and homogenized; rather it would retain its disorder and provide a contrast with the mall—the sacred heart, the great green space—which would gain in stature.

The World's Columbian Exposition in Chicago of 1893, the firm's first large scale involvement in urban planning, indicated the way the American city was perceived.[26] McKim became deeply involved in the enterprise, making over twenty-three trips to Chicago in slightly over two years. He was in many ways the artistic conscience for Daniel Burnham, the grand master of the undertaking, advising him on color, sculpture and architecture. The exposition was far more than a neat orderly ensemble, but was a sprawling mini-city of six hundred acres. The Court of Honor, on which McKim's Agriculture Building stood, was clearly the centerpiece. The Court of Honor alone was a complex environment of different buildings, towers, domes, porticos, columnar orders, bollards, statues, waterways, bridges and gardens. The whole was unified by the use of a white coloring throughout (a plaster of Paris

29.  *Court of Honor, World's Columbian Exposition, Chicago, 1893. From left to right: George B. Post's Manufactures and Liberal Arts Building; Charles B. Atwood's Peristyle; Daniel Chester French's statue of the Republic; McKim, Mead & White's Agricultural Building; and, in immediate foreground, Frederick MacMonnies's Columbian Fountain.*

*31. Vaux-le-Vicomte gardens, with McKim on the steps. Photographed by Frederick Law Olmsted, Jr., for the McMillan Commission, 1901.*

stucco called Staff), a classical style, a consistent cornice height of seventy feet and a rational circulation plan. The Court of Honor was but one segment of the exposition and acted as a civic center. There were two other environments: the more natural and park-like section of the wooded isle on which the Japanese pavilion was placed, and the midway, containing the Ferris wheel, belly dancers and sideshows. As the Court of Honor was analagous to a civic center, then the wooded section was an American suburb, and the midway, an American main street. McKim, Mead & White knew they had to work within all three environments.

McKim, Mead & White were not particularly enthralled with the disharmony of the American city. The three partners worked with various public and private organizations such as the New York Municipal Art Commission and the

*30. Aerial view of Washington, D.C., and the Mall. McMillan Plan, 1902. Rendering by Francis L. V. Hoppin.*

*32. Proposal for Watergate, Lincoln Memorial and bridge to Arlington, Virginia. Washington, D.C., McMillan Commission, 1901. Rendering by Carlton T. Chapman.*

Municipal Art Society, but there was always a certain sense of fatalism about the problems of improving the large city. In 1903 McKim was asked by Mayor Seth Low to participate in a commission to study the New York City parks. McKim declined and explained in a letter that the problems were so complex that unless all the boroughs of New York would be considered, along with "the finding of those competent to deal with the transportation and real estate problems of the city," it would be futile. "The difficulties to be overcome here, are," McKim continued, "so far as the Borough of Manhattan are concerned, insuperable, and with but a few years of breath left to hope for, there are several ways in which I could put in my time more effectively."[27] Earlier, in 1897, he had written to Augustus Saint-Gaudens: "There is only one Paris, and my experience has been, on returning there several times since the war, that one cannot be long there without appreciating the tremendous relief from our purely commercial surroundings, as well as freedom from the unsympathetic noises and crudities of a new civilization. I think I was one of the very first to take advantage of an early trip on the new elevated railroad, when it was started in 1878, and I am sure that as the time passes, it and similar inventions jar more and more upon me. At the present moment nearly every one of our thoroughfares is given over to a new franchise, the sole aim of which is for private gain and apparently without much reference to any other consideration."[28]

The attitude of McKim, Mead & White toward the modern metropolis was analagous to and possibly influenced by the French eighteenth-century theorist Abbe Laugier. In his *Essai sur l'Architecture* (1753), the city is described as follows:

*One must look at a town as a forest. The streets of the one are the roads of the other; both must be cut through in the same way. The essential beauty of a park consists in the great number of roads, their width and their alignment. This, however, is not sufficient: it needs a Le Notre to design the plan for it, someone who applies taste and intelligence so that there is at one and the same time order and fantasy, symmetry and variety, with roads here in the pattern of a star, there in that of a patte d'oie, with a featherlike arrangement in one place, fanlike in another with parallel roads further away and everywhere carrefours of different design and shape. The more variety, abundance, contrast and even disorder in this composition, the greater will be the piquant and delightful beauty of the park. One should not believe that esprit has a place only in higher things. Everything which is susceptible of beauty, everything which demands inventiveness and planning is suitable to set off the imagination, the fire, the verve of a genius. The picturesque can be found in the pattern of a parterre as much as in the composition of a painting.*[29]

The result for McKim, Mead & White was an urban picturesque vision, and they viewed the city as a great forest, where in open spaces such as squares and intersections, temples, statues or other works of art would be placed. A series of special places would be created, like jewels—some large and assertive, others small and hidden—that would provide relief against the audible, visual and physical assault of a commercial civilization. Their methods would be small patches of greenery, such as the few feet of lawn along the Fifth Avenue front of the Metropolitan Club to entire parks, lamp standards strung as pearls on a chain, statues, triumphal arches, street decorations, buildings of different and competing sizes, shapes and stylistic references and, finally, the complete ensemble, the coherent group of buildings such as the university campuses and the Mall in Washington, D.C.

The idea of the urban picturesque was an ever-changing spectacle, to work in small increments providing amenities where possible. They liked, when possible, to provide public seating with statues, such as the General Sherman, or buildings, such as the base of the Boston Public Library. The city would be a series of incidents, almost an architectural museum. For example, on Fifth Avenue at the corners of Thirty-sixth and Thirty-seventh Streets, between 1903 and 1906, Stanford White designed buildings for the Gorham Company and the Tiffany Company that differed significantly from each other and provided points of contrast. The programs for both buildings were similar, though the Gorham had more rental office space. The Gorham, above its great ground-floor arcade carried on Ionic columns, had four floors of almost blank wall surface punctured by windows, then a top level of two stories behind a giant colonnade and, finally, a gigantic projecting cornice of eight feet. The Tiffany Building, on the

33. *General William Tecumseh Sherman Memorial, New York, 1892–1903, by Augustus Saint-Gaudens with base by McKim. In background is the Metropolitan Club, designed by White, 1891–94.*

*34. Gorham Company Building, New York, 1903–06*

other side of Fifth Avenue and a short block away, was entirely different, as an open structure recalling Venetian prototypes. Between the two buildings a dialogue took place, indicating different ways of treating street facades. Importantly, White saw the issue as not simply providing street-level glamour, but maintaining visual interest throughout the entire facade.

A similar changefulness and repertoire of different styles is observable in the firm's work in Naugatuck, Connecticut. The firm designed nine structures between 1885 and 1906 for John Howard Whittemore, a local industrialist. The buildings, for the most part placed around the town green, are not related to each other stylistically, or through materials, but provide a variety of experiences and resemble a small architectural museum.[30] Their relationship is to the town green. The Salem School (1892–94) effectively terminates the major road into town. Above the red-brick school, in 1901–05, the firm designed a new high school, this time more severely classical with a light-colored, granite base surmounted by a colonnade and pavilions of buff brick. It effectively is a temple on an acropolis. On the other side of the green, opposite the schools, the firm placed in 1894 a small, porticoed, pink Milford granite library set back from the street. Between the library and the Victorian Gothic town hall, the firm inserted in a narrow site and placed on the street a small bank (1892–94) built out of light-colored brick. In 1894–95, in center of the green, the firm placed a public drinking fountain, redesigned

35. *Tiffany Company Building, New York, 1903–06*

the walks making them more symmetrical, and located granite bollards around the periphery. And finally, in 1901–03, the original white-frame Congregational Church was replaced by a red-brick and limestone-trimmed Georgian-styled building. The tower is derived from James Gibbs's Saint-Martin-in-the-Fields Church in London. The firm also provided two houses for the Whittemore family located on a road leading out of town, and prepared several other designs that were never erected. Overall, their work in Naugatuck presents not a unity of appearance, style and materials but a varied and picturesque order—the buildings not so much relating to each other, as providing contrast and different points of interest.

This order, combining certain elements of formality but arranged with essentially a picturesque vision, can also be seen in Prospect Park in Brooklyn. Olmsted and Vaux originally designed the park's appendant structure as extensions of the landscaping, using earthtone colors, naturalistic ornament and variated asymmetrical outlines. McKim, Mead & White became the park's official architects about 1889, and over the next twenty years provided new park entrances, gardens and pavilions. Grand Army Plaza provided a monumental entranceway, while the other entrances were more subdued but equally formal. At the south entrance, Frederick MacMonnies's *Horse Tamers* were placed upon large pedestals and connected by balustrades to flanking pavilions. Inside the park a variety of experiences were provided, including a formal rose gar-

38. Plan of Naugatuck, Connecticut:
1. Howard Whittemore Memorial Library   2. Naugatuck National Bank
3. Salem School   4. Fountain and landscaping of green
5. Hillside School   6. Congregational Church

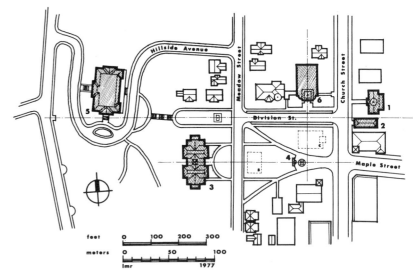

36. Hillside High School,
Naugatuck, Connecticut, 1901–05

37. Howard Whittemore Memorial Library,
Naugatuck, Connecticut, 1891–94

39. Congregational Church, Naugatuck, Connecticut, 1901–03

38

*40. Salem School, Naugatuck, Connecticut, 1892–94.*
*To the right is the corner of the Hillside High School, 1901–05.*

*41. Admiral David Glasgow Farragut Memorial, Madison Square, New York, 1877–81*
*by Augustus Saint-Gaudens and base by Stanford White*

den, the Vale of Cashmere and an exquisite little Corinthian-ordered croquet shelter. These did not mar the park, rather they effectively provided a point of contrast; the classical and formal elements stood out, and alternatively, nature, as in a Claude or a Poussin painting, took on a deeper resonance.

Well over fifty pedestals were designed by McKim, Mead & White for the sculptors Augustus Saint-Gaudens, Frederick MacMonnies and Daniel Chester French. These were collaborations, where the architects worked with the sculptor in securing locations for the proposed piece, and then in concert, designing the pedestal and setting to fit into the specific site. White's base for Saint-Gaudens's *Admiral Farragut* (1877–81) is the most famous. An excedra base with seats carries symbolic figures of *Courage* and *Loyalty* who emerge from the water. The

42. Horse Tamers *by Frederick MacMonnies
and bases by Stanford White.*
*Park Circle entrance, Prospect Park, Brooklyn, 1897.*

calligraphy and figures are Renaissance inspired and set off the naturalistic Farragut, who similarly is descended from fifteenth-century Florentine sculpture. Saint-Gaudens's great *Sherman Victory* statue on Grand Army Plaza at the Fifth Avenue and Fifty-ninth Street entrance to Central Park in New York was originally modeled for an undetermined site. Through the work of McKim, who served on the City Art Commission, the site was finally selected, and McKim and Saint-Gaudens worked out the pedestal. The first sketches called for a pedestal fifteen to eighteen feet high, specifically modeled to provide seating. The entire ensemble and the immediate surrounding pavement, lawn and bushes were part of the design, and were intended to provide an extension of Central Park onto Fifth Avenue, and similarly, the city into the park. A very different intention is apparent with the Colonel Robert Gould Shaw Memorial in Boston. Composed of a large relief of Shaw and his black regiment, the site

43. *Vale of Cashmere with Frederick MacMonnies's* Boy and Duck, *Prospect Park, Brooklyn, 1895–98*

*44. The Bowery Savings Bank, New York, 1893–95*

across from Bulfinch's Boston State House was secured by McKim. Trees provide a backdrop, and the sculpture is located on a terrace which pushes out into the Boston Common. The entire ensemble is richly decorated by surrounds, a fountain, railings and benches, all designed by McKim, with stairs leading up from the Common below. The location and setting is such that while perceivable at a distance, it contains its own small forecourt and is removed from the direct line of traffic. The Shaw Memorial is a quiet spot on a busy street, a hallowed place for remembering a gallant regiment and its leader.[8]

A photograph taken shortly after completion of the Bowery Savings Bank in New York (1895) shows the point of contrast McKim, Mead & White thought their architecture, as works of urban and civic art, ought to make with the surrounding environment. The site was difficult, for it was not a corner, but an L-shaped plot with frontage on both the Bowery and Grand Street. White devised a plan that linked the two sides and created a grand noble interior space. For the exterior and the main entrance on the Bowery, a Roman temple portico was placed. The richly coffered banking vault of the interior extrudes, and the front is lavishly decorated with Greek fret moldings, Corinthian columns and acroteria. Frederick MacMonnies provided the pediment sculpture. The surrounding environment is dismal, and across the front of the bank ran the smoking, belching elevated railroad. Yet the building stands there, a beacon of beauty and aspiration in a harsh environment.

45.  *New York State Building, World's Columbian Exposition, Chicago 1893. White was the building's chief designer.*

**Eclecticism and Design**   A consciousness of history lay at the heart of McKim, Mead & White's architecture; they saw their work as existing in a continuum with previous concerns and solutions. Eclecticism, meaning the selection and usage of styles, motifs and details drawn from a variety of sources, best defines their type of historical usage. In contrast, revivalism—generally connoting the selection of a single style as the basis of design—only defines a portion of their work, such as the High Italian Renaissance Villard houses and the Metropolitan Club. McKim, Mead & White were revivalists within certain styles, but overall they were eclectics, seeking and using the best precedent for the task. Their direction was towards classicism, but a broad-based classicism, drawing upon Greece, Rome, early Christian, Italian, French, English, American, and other Renaissance varieties. To separate the process of eclecticism from the meanings involved is arbitrary, however necessary, if the actual use of the past—creative and otherwise—is to be understood.

The usage of historical precedent by the firm operated in two different ways: first, the type or degree of reference; and second, the method of reference. Type or degree concerns whether the choice is details and motifs, or specific forms and prototypes. In other words, the amplitude of reference—details of ornament or a portico or an entire facade. The Edgar house exhibits an eclecticism of details, the form is only vaguely Georgian and from no specific source, but the details of the widow's walk are

46.  *Villa Medici, Rome*

from Salem, the tall roof from the James River plantations, the chimneys from Carter's Grove or Independence Hall and the portico from Bulfinch. The New York State Building at the World's Columbian Exposition is an eclecticism of form and prototype, the Villa Medici (or the French Academy) in Rome by Annibale Lippi is instantly recognizable as the source, but transformed by making it freestanding, reorganizing the facade and fenestration, adding a prominent frieze, and creating on the roof a terrace from which a subsidiary structure and the towers rise. Eclecticism of form or details existed throughout the firm's life. An early example of eclecticism of form is the Villard houses, while a later example of eclecticism of details is the Pennsylvania Railroad Station, which is

43

47. *"Old House," Newport, Rhode Island. The Bishop Berkeley house, Middletown, Rhode Island, 1729. McKim was assistant editor of* New York Sketch Book of Architecture.

and second, a "scientific eclecticism," where fidelity to the original reference is important. Synthetic eclecticism tends to dominate the work of the Early Period and to be replaced by scientific eclecticism in the periods of Consolidation and High Classical, where liberal quotation and accurate replication is the keynote. In neither synthetic nor scientific eclecticism was exact duplication of the past a goal, rather history was to serve as a catalyst to the imagination, suggesting solutions and as an inspiration to excel.

Synthetic eclecticism is characterized by a juxtaposition and free treatment of details and forms, such as the Tilton house, which combines Queen Anne, American Colonial, Japanese and Tudor motifs. All of the work of the Early Period was conceived of as belonging to a contemporary style such as Queen Anne or modernized Colonial, or combinations of styles. Synthetic eclecticism was not simply a stylistic eclecticism, but could be concerned with transformation of forms, as in Richardson and White's Watts Sherman house, which is a diminution of Richard Norman Shaw's "olde English" manorial houses, such as Leyes Wood or Hopedene. McKim's Bellevue Avenue facade of the Newport Casino is an organized version of a Shavian facade, such as the Tabour Store and Inn at Bedford Park. Also an example of synthetic eclecticism of form is White's own country house, Box Hill, which he enlarged over the years, using the same Queen Anne reiterated gables as in Shaw's work or perhaps Philip Webb's Standen.

The large shingled houses most com-

a completely original creation, with the reference to the past existing in details such as the General Waiting Room, which is a transformed and enlarged tepidarium based on the Baths of Caracalla.

As important in understanding McKim, Mead & White's eclecticism is the method of reference—or how accurately the details and forms are treated—and in this two responses can be distinguished: first, a "synthetic eclecticism," where details and forms are liberally interpreted;

mon in the 1870s and 1880s are examples of synthetic eclecticism and the attempt to create a modernized Colonial style. The huge spreading roofs, which became the archetypal emblems as in the Howells, Tilton and Low houses, were identified as a Colonial feature, which McKim had promoted as early as 1874 in a photograph published in the *New York Sketch Book of Architecture.* McKim commissioned the photograph of the Bishop Berkeley house, ca. 1729, in Middletown, Rhode Island; however, rather than the formal front it was of the long sloping rear roof. In McKim's work the long spreading roofs became so identified that by 1878 William Dean Howells would claim his red roof "is the most colonial feature of all."[31]

The difference between synthetic eclecticism and scientific eclecticism is a matter of method, or approach—how accurately the original source will be treated. It reflects a growing intensity towards the study of the past, common to the turn-of-the-century period, as in McKim's ordering a "squeeze," or a wax impression of the joints of the Erectheum in Athens as a model for laying up "dry" the walls of the Morgan Library.[32] McKim, Mead & White took pride in the accuracy of their treatment of the original source. They paraded their knowledge, education and travels, and in turn brought into question the ability of architects who lacked training and firsthand experience with the past. Synthetic, or loose association with historical models, became *passé,* replaced by a new scientific and scholarly knowledge. The vastly increased knowledge of art

*48. John Andrew house, Boston, 1883–86*

history gave an order to the past, and classified, catalogued, filed and recorded styles, motifs and details. This documentation came in the form of books, of which the firm had as many as twenty-five hundred, and photographs, numbering well into the tens of thousands. Finally, on-site observation was a part, as when McKim posed people for photographs in the ruins of the Baths of Caracalla to observe scale and size.[33] The key point of scientific eclecticism was the recognizable quotation and the accurate

45

and consistent quality of architectural detail. The scientific, somewhat impersonal and overly accurate character of some of McKim, Mead & White's ornamental detail has been commented upon by other critics, and although it may have been a result of the new methods

of terra cotta, fibrous plaster and other machine-age technologies, the high degree of accuracy in hand-cut stone and wood, indicates it was a sought-after quality by the designers.[34] The design of architectural detail was never left to the craftsmen, rather quarter-size, and in many cases full-size, detail drawings would be produced, portraying each dentil, each Roman "V" and every turn of a rope molding.

Three townhouses in the Back Bay of Boston illustrate the firm's development from synthetic to scientific eclecticism. The earliest house, the John Andrew, appeared symmetrical from the front, drawing upon the ubiquitous Boston swell front that first appeared in Federal guise on Beacon Hill about 1805. The swell front is only to the left of the entrance, and what appears to be a duplicate bay to the right emerges as an elliptical tower for turning the corner. The tower is not a Boston Federal or Beacon Hill tradition, but rather a Queen Anne hangover. The division of a limestone base and brick upper walls has precedent with Bulfinch's Federal architecture, but the bricks are long, narrow, buff-colored Roman type, a new import of the 1880s. Detailing of window frames, the awkward Palladian window, the heavy cornice and balustrade, these are Italian Renaissance in origin, not early Boston. The second Back Bay house, the Alexander Cochrane house, is more obviously Beacon Hill, with the single swelling bay, and the window details have a Federal precedent. Yet the heavy pediment over the front door is distinctly Renaissance in origin, though more

*49. Alexander Cochrane house, Boston, 1886–88*

elaborate, and the fourth floor with its string course and brick panels has nothing to do with Boston traditions. With the exception of the large, plate-glass windows, the final Boston work, the J. A. Beebe house of 1890 would almost fit into Beacon Hill. It is a very scholarly adaptation of Boston Federal townhouses.[35] The progression in these townhouses towards an accuracy of details and form indicates the direction of the firm's eclecticism from a synthetic combination of forms and details to an academic and scientific study of the original models and their replication.

Implicit within the direction toward a more recognizable and scientific quotation was the development of an alternative approach to design that differed from the usual Beaux-Arts concentration upon plan. This alternative concentrated upon the form of the building as of primary importance and allowed plan to be fitted in as possible. H. Van Buren Magonigle, a former draughtsman, claimed: "The weak point . . . was their plan. None of them had had that training planning as a science and as the real germ of a design. . . . McKim was the only one to enter the *Ecole des Beaux Arts,* and plan seems never to have touched his consciousness. Both he and White worked from the outside in, conceiving first the exterior appearance of the building, or one front of it, and letting the plan follow and be fitted to it somehow. The relations of the plans and elevations of the Boston Public Library are lamentable and childish."[36] Magonigle overstates the case but he does reveal that plans were frequently second-

*50. J. Arthur Beebe house, Boston, 1888–90*

ary to the exterior form of a building.

Actually, the conflict between exterior form and plan goes back to the methodology of the Ecole des Beaux-Arts. The Beaux-Arts is normally thought of (as by Magonigle) as being ruled by the orthodoxy of the plan; the plan generated spatial volumes and outer forms. Traditionally, the *parti,* or the essence of the idea of a design, was arrived at within a very limited period of time, or *en loge.* This would be presented in an *esquisse,* or drawings of plan, elevation and section. To speedily arrive at a *parti,* a vast knowledge of previous solutions or prototypes had to be maintained in the designer's head. While a certain formula of response existed as far as axis, symmetry, particularization of functions and center,

51. *Bibliothèque Sainte Geneviève, Paris, 1838–50, by Henri Labrouste*

the student was also expected to make appropriate historical references, hence a great emphasis upon architectural history and knowledge of entire buildings, plans, forms and details. Actually, the beginning students' first projects were to copy the orders, ancient fragments and entire buildings.

With such background, the solution to a design problem, whether in an atelier or an office, might as easily be arrived at through form as through plan. Attempting to rapidly formulate a solution for a library, certain prototypical forms such as the Bibliotheque Sainte Geneviève would be referred to, and the *parti* sketches might contain portions of the plan or the form. Similarly, a commission for a New York men's club would entail remembrances of other solutions like the Pall Mall clubs of Sir Charles Barry and the adoption of Renaissance palazzi. Finally, it was an axiom of the

Beaux-Arts that the appearance of a building should reveal its purpose. The interpretation of function could lead to many possibilities, but a knowledge of prototypes provided obvious solutions.

The use of a prototypical form as a source for a *parti* and its elaboration and development can be seen in McKim's Boston Public Library. The Copley Square facade and the front portion of the plan are heavily indebted to Henri Labrouste's Bibliotheque Sainte Geneviève, a building McKim knew well. The source for Labrouste is obviously a Renaissance palazzo, with the *piano noble* serving as the main reading room and stacks located in the basement. McKim used the Sainte Geneviève as a beginning and moved back to the original palazzo form for an interior courtyard. McKim liked to claim that the library had an origin in the Roman Colosseum, perhaps referring to the thickening of the walls and deepening of the reveals of the arches across the front in comparison to the Parisian example.[37] McKim also reduced the number of arches on the front from nineteen to thirteen, lessening the perceivable parts as well as the sprawl. The Boston library is more of a definable unit than the Sainte Geneviève: corners are strengthened, a heavier cornice is used, thicker molding stretches across the front at the main-floor level and at the base, and the building is set up on a podium. Window heads are changed from round to square to further emphasize the ground floor. The single portal of the Parisian example goes through a metamorphosis in McKim's hands to become a triumphal arched entrance vestibule. Ornament and details are more Italian Renaissance in McKim's design, though one decorative element of the Sainte Geneviève is kept: the inscriptions and lists of authors and famous men announce the building's purpose as guardian of culture and make it "readable." The finely detailed deep arches and rondels of the main floor strongly recall Alberti's Tempio Malatestiano. The courtyard arcade is based upon the Cancelleria. In plan, McKim followed Labrouste's scheme of a central entry, hall, staircase up the rear and reading room across the front, but he elaborated and ceremonialized it with more cross axes on both floors. Stacks are located in the back half of the McKim design and specialized libraries and services take up the remainder of the front half. As Magonigle noted, the plan obviously came last and the conflict between the grand processional route into the building and up the stairs, with termination of a diminutive entrance into the reading room, is unsatisfactory, as are the awkward

52. *New York* Herald *Building, 1890–95 and Herald Square with the Sixth Avenue El, photo 1910*

connections to the courtyard and the main third-floor space (the Hall of Religions), which is not even observable on the exterior.

Beginning with Labrouste's design, McKim innovated a solution that returned to the original source of Italian fifteenth- and sixteenth-century palazzi for ideas and forms, but, in the process, became an American freestanding building. The elaborate decorative program with sculptures and murals again had a source in the Sainte Geneviève, but McKim went far beyond and brought into the frame of reference the entire history of printing, the development of knowledge, the legend of the Holy Grail, the world's religions and many other references. McKim added the weight of history and culture to the Boston library making it a new composition.

The New York *Herald* Building is an example of the selection of an exterior form that serves as an envelope and almost completely contradicts the interior. Publisher James Gordon Bennett asked White to design a low-rise building based upon the Doges Palace in Venice. White demurred, probably because New York already had an example with the National Academy of Design, and it was not classical in origin. Instead, White convinced Bennett that the Palazzo del Consiglio in Verona, sometimes attributed to Fra Giacondo, could serve equally well. The Consiglio is a small arcaded facade of multiple rhythms that faces on a piazza. The *Herald* site was trapezoidal, surrounded on all sides by streets. White simplified and stretched out the Consiglio's bays to envelope the *Herald* on all four sides. On the long sides, the general rhythm of the Consiglio is maintained, though with a regularization of openings. Pilasters frame the corner bays, and a continuous open loggia carries a pilaster-enframed upper wall of twin lighted pedimented windows. For the entrance, a different rhythm of two flanking bays of single arches and windows above, sur-

53. *Palazzo del Consiglio, Verona*

round the central loggia of three arches that carry panels for a clock and wind direction and a central window for Bennett's office. The surface cladding was a rich frosting of low-relief terra cotta in buff, yellow and white that regularized and elaborated upon the frescoes in the Consiglio. The interior plan was obviously secondary, a juxtaposition of irregular spaces that contained on the lower floors the more physical activities of the press room, typesetting and delivery, and, on the upper floor, the more cerebral activities of writing and editing. A perfectly circular entrance lobby contrasted with the remainder of the interior, but gave to the visitor a sense of order, the same order that the harmonious exterior gave to the irregular site and the surrounding disorder of the city.

Even when a design was not based upon a specific source from the past, the necessity of providing an ordered exterior image dominated. The Robert Patterson house occupies a polygonal site in Washington, D.C., on Dupont Circle where "P" Street and Massachusetts Avenue converge. The form with the shallow courtyard and loggia creates a recessed space of a diminutive axis against the linear vistas that lead off on all sides. Clad on the exterior in white marble and terra cotta, White used Italian Renaissance references in the ornamentation. The fruit swags, winged putti and escutcheons are strongly reminiscent of the stucco decorations on the Palazzo Spada of 1550, probably by Girolamo da Carpi, with stuccos by Giulio Mazzoni, and the Palazzo Branconio dall Aquila by Raphael of 1515. The interiors

*55. Robert W. Patterson house, Washington, D.C., 1900–03*

were equally impressive; White selected antique fragments and furniture from his own collection and had sent down a selection of pictures from a New York gallery. A repertory of different styles was selected for the different spaces and then turned over to such decorating firms as Alland & Sons for the ball and reception rooms; Marcotte & Company for the library; Tiffany Studios for the dining room; Hayden and Company for the halls and conservatory; and A. H. Davenport & Company provided much of the furniture.

The importance of the exterior over the plan can be seen in an exchange of letters between White and Patterson, where the latter's concern with large entertainment spaces was uppermost and White's concern with the exterior was paramount. Replying to a question on a preliminary plan with a front courtyard, White claimed it was "just for looks and second, to save some money on the cost of the house."[38] Three days later White sent Patterson two plans for consideration and noted if he had any preference; "The best thing to do is to try them at once and see which works up in the best elevation and plan, and adopt this."[39] A week later, still being pressed by Patterson, White replied: "I have been working hard over the house, but none of the new plans or schemes compares with the design already made. The old design as you can see by the new sketch has a light and rather joyous character, and the court gives it decided originality, whereas by bringing the entrance out to the street, the house apparently is greatly increased in size (and cost) and becomes

56. *Patterson house, detail*

much more commonplace."[40]

In this triumph of form over plan, of recognizable imagery over function, it was apparent his concern was the public nature of architecture. The commission, whether a private house, a commercial building or a civic structure, had a public responsibility not simply in the area of "good design," but to present an image of the cultural heritage and accomplishments of Americans.

**Meaning**  Public in the sense of having recognizable historical imagery, the architecture of McKim, Mead & White was replete with meanings that ranged from the self-congratulatory to the universal. The Italian Renaissance palazzo transmuted into houses for American robber barons provided an obvious analogy with the accomplishments of the merchant princes of Rome, Florence and Venice. The triumphal arches used to commemorate the centennial of Washington's inauguration as president or the soldiers and sailors of the Union in the Civil War added the lineage of association with other great events and themes in world history. The Washington, D.C., Plan of 1901–02 on which McKim worked (along with Daniel Burnham, Augustus Saint-Gaudens and Frederick Law Olmsted, Jr.) can be interpreted as a reassertion of Major Pierre Charles L'Enfant's original 1791 scheme and the triumph of the Beaux-Arts. In a broader context it attempted to associate the American capital with the great formal planning schemes of European centers of power and to create an American forum of vast spaces and distances within which the past, the present and future would be united in a constant ceremonial affirmation of national greatness. McKim, Mead & White consciously investigated architectural imagery and form with the belief that it could play a significant role in molding and reforming society, in creating standards for a great civilization.

The gulf between the crass demands of the marketplace for a historical legitimacy and the idealism of architecture as a civilizing vehicle indicates the origins of the partners within the intellectual elite of the pre-Civil War period and the changes that occurred to that elite in the latter-nineteenth century. They grew up hearing discussions and arguments over slavery, Verdi and Whitman. Crucial to their development was the idea of "culture" and "civilization" and the question of what America's role should be. This idealistic argument was to continue after the war and through the later-nineteenth and early-twentieth centuries, though somewhat shifting with the changing circumstances of growing industrial and commercial enterprises, increased wealth and leisure time, swelling centers of population, expanding government accompanied by frequent corruption, improved education, and new aspirations for culture and its institutions. That Charles McKim, William Mead and Stanford White, as sons of families who had essentially dealt in ideas, would choose careers as architects indicates the more materialistic and object-centered climate of the turn-of-the-century period.

Materialism and self-aggrandizement were always present in McKim, Mead & White's work, yet also present was an idealistic belief that through architecture the general level of culture and civilization could be raised. McKim, in particular, liked to quote Thomas Jefferson's exhortation that the reproduction of European buildings in the United States was a means of educating American public taste in architecture.[41]

Contributing to the partners' architectural beliefs were a number of writers, beginning about mid-century, who argued that architecture and the arts were rep-

57. *Proposal for Union Square in front of the Capitol Building, Washington, D.C., by the McMillan Commission. Rendering by C. Graham.*

resentative of a nation or a people. As an outgrowth of nineteenth-century historiography and the discovery that the arts, and architecture in particular, revealed characteristics of a country, there occurred the attempt to identify national styles, or import foreign styles claiming they were within the lineage of the country and had specific associations worthy of replication. As educated young men, the partners could be expected to have read John Ruskin and his claim: "It has been my endeavor to show . . . how every form of noble architecture is in some sort the embodiment of the Polity, Life, History, and the Religious faith of nations."[42] This line of reasoning would be paraphrased by Owen Jones who, in *The Grammar of Ornament* (1858), wrote: "Architecture is the material expression of the wants, the faculties, and the sentiments of the age in which it is created."[43] Practically all the mid-century theorists expressed similar concepts; however, the most important for young Americans attending the Ecole des Beaux-Arts would be Eugene Emmanuel Viollet-le-Duc. Viollet-le-Duc, though not trained at the Ecole, was a severe critic of its training and exerted a substantial influence on McKim, who attempted to study with him and translated portions of his writings. To Viollet-le-Duc, "Each nation, or to speak more correctly, each center of civilization . . . has . . . a genius of its own which must not be disregarded; and it is because during the last three centuries we have too often failed to appreciate our own genius, that our arts . . . have become hybrid."[44] This concept of the inspired role of race, or nation,

had been developed by his friend Hippolyte Taine, who became the lecturer in history at the Ecole succeeding Viollet-le-Duc's short tenure in 1863.

For the United States, with a strong nationalistic and inferiority complex, the notion of architecture as an exponent of civilization received confirmation from writers such as James Jackson Jarves: "Each civilized race, ancient or modern, has incarnated its own æsthetic life and character in definite forms of architecture. . . . To get at the prevailing life motive of any epoch, we must read its architecture, as well as its literature."[45] The first English language translation of Viollet-le-Duc was by the American architect Henry Van Brunt, who wrote in his 1875 introduction: "As all history may be read by an intelligent observation of the monuments of the past, . . . it is certainly important for us to see to it that *our* civilization is having a proper exponent in our monuments." The answer for Van Brunt was eclecticism: "We Americans occupy a new country, having no inheritance of ruins. . . . All the past is ours. [The] essential distinction between the arts of primitive barbarism and those of civilization is that, while the former are original and independent, and consequently simple, the latter must be retrospective, naturally turning to tradition and precedent, and are therefore complex."[46] The inaugural issue of the first professional architectural journal in the United States, the *American Architect and Building News* for January 1876, announced: "We are overwhelmed with the abundance of precedent at our hands, and help ourselves from all sides. . . . We have no style which is a long inheritance to use, as the Renaissance is to the French, or the Gothic to the English . . . whether eclecticism is desirable or not, the tendency of our people toward it is too strong to be resisted."[47] Further defining the problem the editors wrote in a later issue: "We have to create an architecture, and we are expected to furnish it readymade. We are not given three or four centuries to develop it in . . . academic conservatism we have none, old traditions and standards we have none."[48]

McKim, Mead & White began their architectural careers contemporaneously with this dialogue over the direction, or rather lack of direction, in American architecture. They would create an academy, standards and traditions, but their essential heritage was that of eclecticism. Harry Desmond and Herbert Croly, writing nearly thirty years later on the firm, asserted: "The only habit of thought which Americans have had in relation to architecture is that of imitation."[49] Accepting eclecticism as the basis, the question then became what should be imitated, why Italian Renaissance as in the Gorham Building and not Italian Gothic? Why English Georgian as in the Twombly house and not English medieval? The answer lay in the perceived association of the style by Americans, and in the principles of architectural order and classicism. The solution, as we have seen in the periods of the firm's development, was not clear-cut at first; they can be seen exploring a variety of directions, including even the medieval. Yet a clear bias towards classical details

and forms can be seen from the very beginning.

Late in life McKim reflected upon his first visit in 1869 to England, and "the discovery of a strange familiarity in the appearance of things, and the sense of not being after all so far from home."[50] The similarity was, of course, between the forms and details of English Renaissance and Georgian architecture and what could be found in the Colonial and Federal remains of Boston, Newport, Salem, Philadelphia and other early American cities. That this architecture was being "revived" by the Queen Anne architects and seen in England as a na-

*58. Miss Dep. Cary house, Lenox, Massachusetts, 1878.
Designed by McKim in partnership with Mead and Bigelow.*

tional style could not escape him. Consequently the researches by McKim into the American colonial past with photographs and the "celebrated" sketching and measuring trip he took with Mead, Bigelow and White in 1877 along the north shore of Massachusetts was an attempt to create an American architectural heritage, just as also was his call for "antiquarian architects."[51] Emerging first as an eclecticism of details merged with the Queen Anne as in the Moses Taylor house, by the late 1870s McKim had produced a full-scale modernized Colonial or Shingle Style, as in the Cary house. In the early 1880s, more thorough knowledge of the American past led McKim and his partners into more firmly historicizing works, as the Appleton house, which recalled eighteenth-century works.

The break that certain historians claim lies between the work of the Shingle Style and work inspired by the Italian Renaissance does not exist; all McKim, Mead & White's designs are concerned with creating evocative images. What is different is the realization on their part that the American image was both of necessity and reality far more complex than the seventeenth- and eighteenth-century Colonial examples. Furthermore, the shingled modernized Colonial appeared as a resort style, possibly suitable for the country and suburbs, but not for the modern metropolis. Certain American idioms such as the Boston Federal would provide only a partial solution; needed was a wider approach which became obvious in the mid-1880s with the Villard houses and the Boston Public

Library. Acceptance of these designs as American resulted from a new perception that the origins of America were laid in the period of the Renaissance. Out of the Italian Renaissance and its sources from Greece and Rome had come the other European manifestations: French, German and English Renaissance; American Colonial; Bulfinch Federal; Jeffersonian Roman and the Greek Revival—a tradition McKim, Mead & White were reviving.

From the mid-1870s, there was a marked increase in knowledge and appreciation of the Italian Renaissance as a high point of Western achievement, and a period to be emulated. In the United States, by the early 1880s, references began to suggest an equivalent American Renaissance. American arts, architecture and culture were perceived as experiencing a rebirth through their reliance upon the original European manifestations.[52] Sentiments such as those expressed by Harry Desmond and Herbert Croly regarding the work of McKim, Mead & White are revealing: "Of all modern peoples we are most completely the children of the Renaissance; and it would be fatal for us to deny our parentage. In our architectural practice we should in the beginning expressly affirm this parentage, rather than evade or deny it."[53]

The Desmond and Croly review was the most substantial and sympathetic review the firm received during the lifetime of the major partners, and the references made to the philosophical ideals embodied within the work make apparent the perceived connections with the

Renaissance.

*Given the situation as it was and is in this country, cannot a very strong case be made in favor of a conscious, persistent attempt to adapt the architecture of the Renaissance to American uses? As a source of available architectural forms they were and are well adapted to our needs. They were familiar to the traveler and educated American public, and appealed to the somewhat florid American taste. They were, comparatively speaking modern buildings. . . . They had assumed during the best years of the Renaissance many different practical types and aesthetic forms, and this is an enormous advantage. . . . They were . . . endowed with the necessary historical sanction and glamor.*

*The value of the architecture of the Renaissance to the modern American architect is, however, more than a matter of mere availability. Can we not claim with the Renaissance an intimate intellectual kinship? The word Renaissance stands for a group of political, social and educational ideas, which although profoundly modified by the historical experience of the last four hundred years, have not yet spent their force. Intellectually it was based on a renewed faith in mankind and in the power of men to act and think for themselves, and the return to classical antiquity which marked its earlier phases was the outcome of an attempt to find an historical basis and sanction for this humanism. . . . The Renaissance as a philosophical and moral ideal is receiving its most sincere and thoroughgoing expression in the United States. . . . Just as the first children of the Renaissance sought to enrich and strengthen their own faith in mankind by assimilating the cul-*

*ture and the art of classical antiquity, so must we keep in touch with the traditional source of our intellectual, moral and political ideals by assimilating what we can of the culture and art both of the Renaissance and of Greece and Rome.*[54]

Accepting the Renaissance and its classical basis would provide for Americans a cultural reference and meaning; the need for a new language or a specifically American expression as Sullivan and Wright were claiming was not a viable alternative. To McKim, as the most public spokesman for the firm, classicism meant a recognized language of architecture, or as he said in an address before the American Institute of Architects: "Architecture is the oldest of the arts. Its principles were developed early in the history of the race, its laws were formulated long before the Christian era; and its most exquisite flowers bloomed under skies that fostered the production of beauty. Succeeding ages have had their special problems calling for special adaptions . . . until there has grown up a vast universal language of architecture." The value of studying the past followed naturally and brought McKim to his major point: "Purpose and location change with each problem; and happy is he who can satisfy those two requirements without being called upon also to invent the language in which he speaks."[55]

The broad latitude of this cultural and architectural interpretation allowed virtually any classical style to be adopted as American: the Tiffany & Company store was a modified version of the Palazzo Grimani in Venice by Sanmicheli; Robinson

59

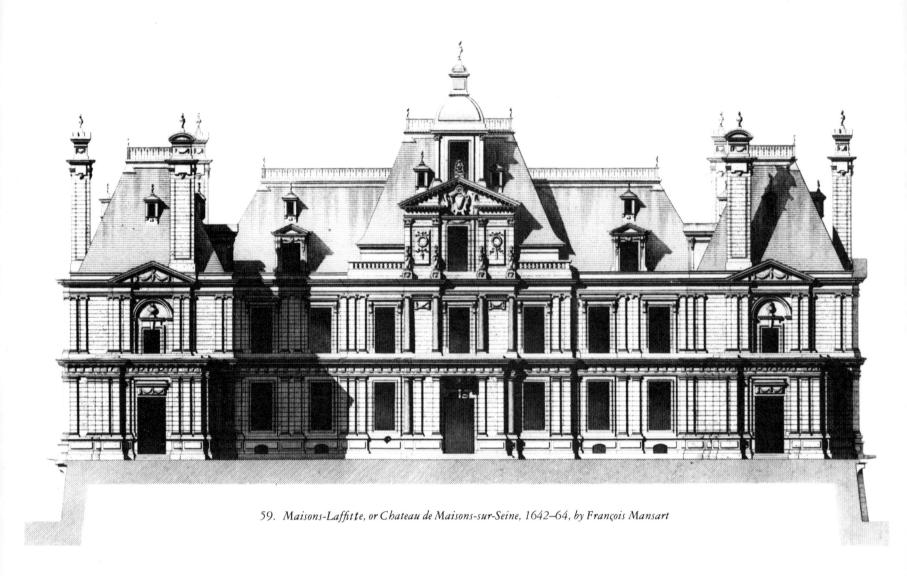

59.  *Maisons-Laffitte, or Chateau de Maisons-sur-Seine, 1642–64, by François Mansart*

Hall at Harvard was a gloss on the older buildings of Harvard Yard; the Knickerbocker Trust Company was an enlarged Hellenistic temple; and the State Savings Bank in Detroit was reminiscent of Alberti's Tempio Malatestiano. Of course, none of these buildings were exact duplicates of their sources, they were modern structures of their time. The Army War College in Washington, D.C., while obviously indebted to Roman classicism for the forms and details, was an entirely new creation. The great barrel vaults, the thermae windows, the repeated piers of the main building all spoke an understandable language. It symbolized both the American connections with the past, and also the triumph of the new world over the old. The connections with Roman imperialism were not unnoted. White, when reproached for his omnivorous collecting of old-world art and antiquities, "defended his actions by saying that in the past dominant nations had always plundered works of art from their predecessors; that America was taking a leading place among nations and had therefore, the right to obtain art wherever she could."[56]

The success of portraying America as the heir of the great ages of classical architecture can be seen in the clientele of McKim, Mead & White—not simply the wealthy patrons but their demands and reactions as well. The instructions of Katherine Mackay to Stanford White are revealing: "I have decided to begin on those plans at once so will you express me as soon as you get this, some books about and drawings of Louis XIV Châteaux. There [sic] severe style preferred. Also hall Henri II (French), staircases Henri II." Three days later another letter arrived from Mrs. Mackay: "The plan where the sides project is what I meant. I have made notes on it to give you points. I do mean a very severe house. The style of the full front view of the Maisons-Laffitte comes closest to what I mean. And even that has the windows too ornate to suit us."[57] Katherine Mackay would continue with ideas for the plan and other specific suggestions. White based his design upon her request, though with modifications such as the doorway, which was drawn from the Hotel de Montescot at Chartres as published in Claude Sauvageot's, *Palais, Châteaux, Hotels et Maisons du France du XVᵉ au XVIIIᵉ Siecles* (1867). Katherine Mackay was an extreme case in her exactness of request, but by every indication it was evident that she knew exactly what she wanted, and with her husband created one of the largest complete American country estates, so impressive that Edward VII, the Duke of Windsor, claimed the lavishness and appointments were beyond anything in England.[58]

A letter by Samuel A. B. Abbott, president of the Board of Trustees of the Boston Public Library, to his architect, Charles McKim, revealed the challenge of the past, and the belief that a modern equivalent was possible:

*I think that if you could go over the same ground you would be satisfied with your work on the Library, for if I am not mistaken it will hold its own beside any of the great works of the great architects of the Renaissance. . . . I paid particular attention to the Chancelleria, the Farnese, and the Strozzi palaces, because you have talked so much of them; and I feel that your work will rank with them.*[59]

At the death of White in 1906 and of McKim in 1909, even as late as the death of Mead in 1928, opinion—both public and architectural—ranked McKim, Mead & White on the level of Alberti, Bramanti, Le Vaux, Mansart, Jones and Wren. Beginning in the 1930s, their reputations fell to the level of clever, but insidious, imitators. Then, in the late 1960s, their standing began to rise again. Each generation finds a new use for the past and creates a new interpretation. It is debatable whether this recent interest in McKim, Mead & White is simply the recognition of the intrinsic quality of the work, or merely a nostalgia for a period of supreme architectural confidence. Behind the brilliance of their architectural solutions (and the obvious failure of others) lie two issues—they committed themselves to a specific architectural order and that commitment arose from their perception of their culture and their clients. Their eclecticism was certainly self-serving for both them and their clients, but apt was the equation of Roman grandeur for Pennsylvania Station, the Renaissance Medici for J. P. Morgan's library, and the High

61. *Ancien Hôtel de Montescot, Chartres, entree de l'hôtel*

60. *Mackay house, doorway*

Georgian for Harvard University. Their architecture was not simply a reaction to the complex of ideas that formed the American Renaissance—they were its creators. Their turn to the language of classicism and its various stylistic and nationalistic manifestations was an attempt to impose a system of order upon American architecture. A measure of their success is the vituperation and venom it took to overturn their architectural solution, and the relatively short life of the replacement.

If culture and architecture have a relationship, then the last fifty years have been a period of a loss of confidence. The question is whether architects can envision a culture with the same confidence, stature and humor as did McKim, Mead & White. They issued a challenge and that challenge still remains to be met.

[1] Royal Cortissoz, "Some Critical Reflections on the Architectural Genius of Charles F. McKim," *The Brickbuilder* XIX, No. 2 (February 1910): 35–36.

[2] Charles H. Reilly, "The Modern Renaissance in American Architecture," *Journal of the Royal Institute of British Architects* Series 3, vol. 17 (June 25, 1910): 635.

[3] W, "A letter from New York," *American Architect and Building News* 2, No. 105 (December 29, 1877): 419. "W" does not use quotation marks, but he is obviously quoting McKim.

4 H. Siddons Mowbray recounting conversation with McKim, October 1897, in Charles Moore, *The Life and Times of Charles Follen McKim* (Boston and New York: Houghton Mifflin Co., 1929), p. 260.

5 Leland Roth, *McKim, Mead & White: A Building List* (New York: The Garland Press, 1979) lists 945 commissions for the years 1870–1919, but this does not include numerous remodelings.

6 H. Van Buren Magonigle, "A Half Century of Architecture 3" *Pencil Points* 15 (March 1934): 116.

7 Lawrence Grant White, *Sketches and Designs by Stanford White* (New York: The Architectural Book Co., 1920), 17.

8 Magonigle, "A Half Century," 117.

9 Letter, Whitelaw Reid to Stanford White, August 19, 1890. Reid Papers, Library of Congress; and Mowbray in Moore, *McKim,* 262.

10 Moore, *McKim,* app. II, "Office Role of McKim, Mead & White" lists 573 office personnel as having been employed between approximately 1878 and 1915.

11 Letter, Stanford White to Charles T. Barney, September 18, 1901, The New-York Historical Society.

12 "Correction," *Art Age* 3 (January 1886): 100; and Letter, Charles McKim to President Roosevelt, July 11, 1902, Library of Congress.

13 William Mitchell Kendall, "Letter to Royal Cortissoz," *The Architectural Record* 66 (July 1929): 18.

14 Moore, *McKim,* 49.

15 Letter, Joseph Morril Wells to Cass Gilbert, July 30, 1884, Library of Congress. William Shopsin and Mosett Broderick, *The Villard Houses: Life Story of a Landmark* (New York: The Viking Press, 1980), contains some analysis of this controversy which differs significantly from above.

16 "The Metcalfe Residence . . . ," *Buffalo Real Estate & Builders Monthly.* Quoted in Francis Kowsky, "A Building in the 'Early Colonial' Style by McKim, Mead and White," *Little Journal* 4, No. 1 (November 1980): 2–11.

17 Vincent Scully, Jr., *The Shingle Style and The Stick Style,* rev. ed. (New Haven: Yale University Press, 1971), 139.

18 George William Sheldon, *Artistic Country Seats* (New York: D. Appleton & Co., 1886–87) I: 23.

19 "Correspondence," *American Architect and Building News* 2, No. 102 (December 9, 1877): 394.

20 Letter, Wells to Gilbert, July 30, 1884, Library of Congress.

21 Bruce Price, "The Suburban House" in *Homes in City and Country,* ed. Russel Sturgis (New York: Charles Scribner's & Sons, 1893), 87.

22 Francecso Passanti, "Columbia University," *Journal of the Society of Architectural Historians* XXXVI (May 1977): 69–84.

23 Carroll L. V. Meeks, "Picturesque Eclecticism," *The Art Bulletin* 32 (September 1950): 226–35; and Buford

24 Edward Bellamy, *Looking Backward, 2000–1887* (New York: Pocket Books, 1957), 30. On the City Beautiful see: Richard Guy Wilson, Dianne Pilgrim and Richard Murray, *The American Renaissance, 1876–1917* (Brooklyn and New York: The Brooklyn Museum and Pantheon Press, 1979), ch. 6 and *passim;* Jon A. Peterson, "The City Beautiful Movement: Forgotten Origins and Lost Meanings," *Journal of Urban History* 2 (August 1976): 415–34; and Mel Scott, *American City Planning Since 1890* (Berkeley: University of California Press, 1971).

25 United States Senate Committee on the District of Columbia, *Report of the Senate Committee on the District of Columbia on the Improvement of the Park System of the District of Columbia* Senate Report No. 166, 57th Congress, 1st Session (Washington, D.C.: Government Printing Office, 1902). See also, John Reps, *Monumental Washington* (Princeton: Princeton University Press, 1967); and Richard Guy Wilson, "Renaissance in the Prairie," *Inland Architect* 24 (April 1980): 5–8.

26 There is much literature on the Exposition, see: David F. Burg, *Chicago's White City of 1893* (Lexington: University Press of Kentucky, 1976).

27 Letter, McKim to Charles Moore, January 8, 1903, Library of Congress.

28 Letter, McKim to Augustus Saint-Gaudens, December 6, 1897, Library of Congress.

29 Marc-Antoine Langier, *Essay on Architecture* (Los Angeles: Hennesy & Ingals, 1977), 128.

30 A. C. David, "An Architectural Oasis," *The Architectural Record* 19 (February 1906): 135–44; and Leland M. Roth, "Three Industrial Towns by McKim, Mead & White," *Journal of The Society of Architectural Histories* XXXVIII (December 1979): 317–47.

31 Letter, William Dean Howells to William Bigelow, February 25, 1878, Amherst College, Amherst, Mass. The Bishop Berkeley house appeared in, *The New York Sketch Book of Architecture* 1, No. 12 (December 1874): 45. See also, Richard Guy Wilson, "The Early Work of Charles F. McKim," *Winterthur Portfolio* 13 (Fall 1979): 235–67.

32 Letter, Charles F. McKim to Mr. Gorham Stevens, December 14, 1903, Library of Congress.

33 Moore, *McKim,* 275.

34 William Jordy, *American Buildings and Their Architects: Progressive and Academic Ideals at the Turn of the Twentieth Century* (Garden City: Doubleday & Co., 1972), vol. 3: 348; Reilly, "The Modern Renaissance in American Architecture," 633; and Peter Smithson, "The Fine and the Folk: An Essay on McKim, Mead and White and the American Tradition," *Architectural Review* 135 (August 1965): 394–97.

35 Bainbridge Bunting, *Houses of Boston's Back Bay* (Cambridge: Harvard University Press, 1967), 326–27.

36 H. Van Buren Magonigle, "A Half Century of Architecture 4" *Pencil Points* 15 (May 1934): 224.

37 Moore, *McKim,* 66.

38 Letter, Stanford White to Mrs. Robert Patterson, January 21, 1901, Avery Architectural Library, Columbia University.

39 Letter, Stanford White to Mrs. Robert Patterson, January 24, 1901, Avery Library.

40 Letter, Stanford White to Mrs. Robert Patterson, February 2, 1901, Avery Library.

41 Henry W. Desmond and Herbert Croly, "The Work of Messrs. McKim, Mead & White," *The Architectural Record* 20 (September 1906): 217.

42 John Ruskin, *The Seven Lamps of Architecture* (London: J. Neal, 1849), 183.

43 Owen Jones, *The Grammar of Ornament* (London: Bernard Quaritch, 1858), 5.

44 Eugene Emmanuel Viollet-le-Duc, *Discourses on Architectures,* trans. B. Bucknall (New York: Grove Press, 1959 [1889]), II: 244.

45 James Jackson Jarves, *The Art Idea* (New York: Hurd & Houghton, 1864), 95, 286.

46 Henry Van Brunt, "Translator's Introduction . . . ," rep. in, Van Brunt, *Architecture and Society,* ed. W. A. Coles (Cambridge: Harvard University Press, 1969), 103, 106.

47 "The Need of Unity," *American Architect and Building News* 1 (January 1, 1876): 3.

48 "Eclecticism in Architecture," *American Architect and Building News* 1 (January 15, 1876): 18.

49 Desmond and Croly, "The Work of Messrs. McKim, Mead & White," 218.

50 "Charles F. McKim's Speech on Receiving the King's Medal," in Moore, *McKim,* 238.

51 *Ibid.,* 41. See also, Richard Guy Wilson, "American Architecture and the Search for a National Style in the 1870s," *Nineteenth Century* 3 (Autumn 1977): 74–80.

52 Wilson, Pilgrim and Murray, *American Renaissance;* Joy Wheeler Dow, *American Renaissance: A Review of Domestic Architecture* (New York: Wm. T. Comstock & Co., 1904); and Howard Mumford Jones, "The Renaissance and American Origins," *Ideas in America* (Cambridge: Harvard University Press, 1945).

53 Desmond and Croly, "The Work of Messrs. McKim, Mead & White," 226.

54 *Ibid.,* 222–26.

55 Charles F. McKim, "Address of the President," 36th Annual Convention of the AIA (1902) Washington, D.C., typescript, McKim Collection, New York Public Library.

56 White, *Sketches and Designs,* 24–25.

57 Letters, Katherine MacKay to Stanford White, July 24 and July 27 (1899), The New-York Historical Society; see also, Lawrence Wodehouse, Stanford White and the MacKays of *Winterthur Portfolio* 11 (1976): 213–33.

58 Edward, Duke of Wales, *A King's Story* (New York and London: G. P. Putnam's Sons, 1951).

59 Letter, Samuel A. B. Abbott to Charles F. McKim, November 28, 1889, Library of Congress.

**Prescott Hall Butler House**
**"By the Harbour"**
**St. James, New York**
**ca. 1871–76**

Charles McKim designed the Butler house prior to his partnerships with William Mead, William Bigelow or Stanford White. The exact date of the Butler house is uncertain; McKim's biographer lists it as 1871, however, the date may be about 1876.[1] No matter the date, the design was an extraordinary tour-de-force for the young McKim and an exciting premonition of his later work, for it directly foreshadowed the Howells, McCormick, Tilton and Low houses. Butler was a Harvard classmate of McKim's and a lawyer in the New York law firm of Joseph Choate. The house was designed as a summer cottage for Butler's young wife, Cornelia Smith, of nearby Smithtown. (Stanford White would marry her sister, Bessie Smith, in 1884, and his summer house, "Box Hill," was a few hundred yards distant.)

McKim's original design has been somewhat altered. The service wing was originally only a single story in height and somewhat shorter. Under a large gable McKim subsumed most of the features, except for the chimneys and dormers. The English Queen Anne covering of hung tiles over a brick base were translated into wood shingles over a clapboard base. The windows and fenestration were asymmetrically composed and yet balanced. The interior has been greatly altered and judgments must be

63. *Elevation, possibly by White, ca. 1884. Watercolor on paper.*

tentative, yet apparently the house was bisected by a straight-through living hall with a fireplace, and the sitting room was pierced by a freestanding fireplace.

[1] Charles Moore, *The Life and Times of Charles Follen McKim* (Boston and New York: Houghton Mifflin, 1929), 38–39 and 318. A letter, Bert Fenner to Lawrence S. Butler, December 10, 1912, The New-York Historical Society gives the date as 1872.

64. *Plan*

65. *Fireplace inglenook in library, with a Queen Anne fan motif in the mantel*

66. *Dining room*

## William Dean Howells House "Redtop"
90 Somerset Street
Belmont, Massachusetts
1877–78

Designed for William Mead's sister and brother-in-law, Elinor and William Dean Howells, the house was intended as a summer retreat from the pressures of the Boston literary community. To the house during the Howells' years of residence, 1878–82, friends such as Samuel Clemons, Henry James and others would come. The house was one of the earliest works of the newly formed McKim, Mead & Bigelow firm. Surviving letters indicate that Charles McKim was the chief designer.[1]

An initial scheme was drawn up by McKim before any site visit and swiftly rejected by Elinor: "The magnificent view is towards Boston, directly east." In turn, McKim visited the site and with the Howells worked out a tightly controlled plan gathered under a large gable with vistas to the south and east. Inevitably, changes were introduced: a sitting room replaced the porch across the front, shingles were added to the gable, and more elaborate interior detailing was selected. Throughout the nine months of construction (occupied July 1878), Bigelow and Mead made inspection trips, but they deferred to McKim for most design decisions.[2] Set on a red brick base with redwood shingles and surrounded by red Jimsonweed, the house acquired the name Redtop.

Organized around a central hall, the wide doorways, the backlighted stairs and the continuous moldings and plate rails gave the sense of a broad expansion of space. Interior detailing combined Queen Anne and Colonial motifs; the library with the inglenook resembled the Queen Anne work of W. E. Nesfield. The dining-room mantel and moldings looked old-fashioned to Elinor, and she wrote approvingly: "The dining room looks 200 years old." The interior was a success with one exception, an awkward butler's pantry.[3]

The exterior design represented McKim's return to the clear geometric form of the Butler house; the uncomfortable picturesqueness of the mid-1870s had disappeared. Detailing was minimal—smooth brick quoins and the turned porch posts were subordinated to the triangular shape of the gable. To eyes of the 1870s, McKim had designed a Colonial Revival house. William Dean Howells wrote: "The red roof (pray say to Mr. McKim) is the most Colonial feature of all," and he added, Mrs. Howells called it a "definite McKimism."[4]

68. *Plan*

[1] Not surprisingly, Howell's biographers have always assumed Mead to be the architect of Redtop. See, Edwin H. Cady, *The Road to Realism: The Early Years 1837–1885 of William Dean Howells* (Syracuse, N.Y.: Syracuse University Press, 1956), 199, 208; and *Life in Letters of William Dean Howells,* ed. Mildred Howells, 2 vols. (Garden City: Doubleday, Doran & Co., 1928), 1:244. Recent scholarship has corrected this misinterpretation and added light to the entire commission. See, Ginette de B. Merril, "Redtop and the Belmont Years of W. D. Howells and His Family," *Harvard Library Bulletin* XXVIII (January 1980): 33–57; and Richard Guy Wilson, "The Early Work of Charles F. McKim: Country House Commissions," *Winterthur Portfolio* 14 (Fall 1979): 235–67. Surviving letters are in the William R. Mead Collection, Amherst College, Amherst, Mass.

[2] No plans exist for the Howells house, but there is an early unidentified sketch that is probably a preliminary drawing in The New-York Historical Society. Letters, Elinor Howells to Mead, November 22, December 4, December 5, December 17, 1877, January 17, 1878 and "Account of Extras," Amherst College. Elinor Howells to Mead, November 22, December 4, 1877, June 15, July 3, 1878 and Meyers (contractor) to McKim, Mead & Bigelow, March 25, 1878, Amherst College.

[3] Letters, Elinor Howells to Mead, July 3, 1878; Elinor Howells complained heartily about the pantry, Howells to Mead, November 11, 1877, Amherst College.

[4] Letters, Howells to Bigelow, February 25, 1878, Amherst College.

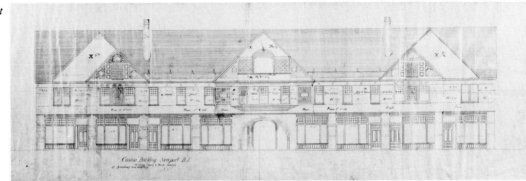

69. *Bellevue Avenue elevation. The different letters and numbers on the upper floors indicate the various shapes and sizes of shingles. Ink on linen.*

**Newport Casino**
**Bellevue Avenue**
**Newport, Rhode Island**
**1879–81**

In the 1870s, an entertainment pavilion known as the Casino appeared on the American resort scene. Writing in 1886, George William Sheldon claimed: "As a source of aesthetic pleasure, the country clubhouse in the United States is scarcely more than eight years old. Its beginning may be traced to the Newport Casino—designed by Messrs. McKim, Mead & White."[1]

The idea of a casino for Newport had been talked about for several years; however, in the summer of 1879, James Gordon Bennett, Jr., smarting from snubs by "polite" society for his uncouth behavior (urinating in a fireplace in front of his fiancée), brought the idea to reality while seeking revenge. Bennett was the heir of the New York *Herald* and well-known for wild, impetuous and gener-

ally intoxicated behavior. In August 1879 Bennett challenged a visiting British Army-office friend to ride a horse into the staid and prestigious Newport Reading Room. A few days later, the Newport *Mercury* reported that Bennett had purchased land on Bellevue Avenue across from his own house with the intention of building a "new club house" for Newport summer fun. The *Mercury* continued: "We further understand that Mr. Bennett has been led to take this step by reason of a dismissal of a friend from the Newport Reading Room for a clear violation of the rules of that institution."[2] Bennett hoped to show how society really preferred scandal and entertainment rather than proper behavior—they would follow him where he went. A limited stock company was formed, and a short while later Charles McKim arrived in Newport to inspect the site and discuss plans.[3] Nathan Baker was selected as the builder and construction began in January 1880 and by July, the doors were opened to the public. The grounds and outbuildings were not

71. *Courtyard*

72. *Courtyard*

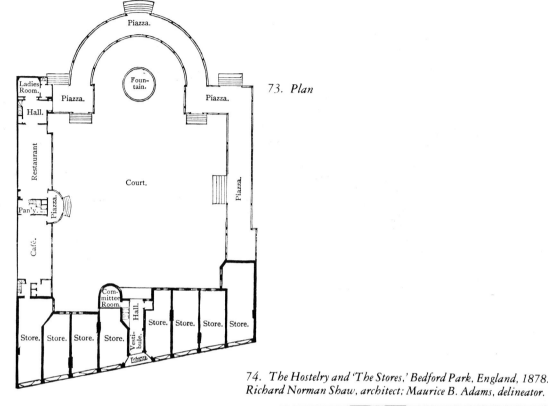

73. *Plan*

complete until the summer of 1881. The Casino contained conversation and lounging rooms, a restaurant, a billiard room, a theater, piazzas for strolling and tennis courts. Also included were guest rooms for bachelors; however, these proved impracticable and were altered into club rooms. In 1881 the Casino was the site of the First National Lawn Tennis Tournament.

Most of the planning of the Casino and the Bellevue Avenue facade, shown in the drawing, can be attributed to Charles McKim. Stanford White certainly contributed some details, as well as portions of the courtyard. The main front had a ground floor of shops and on the upper floors there were entertainment spaces. The large central arch gave access to the upper floors and also to the court and tennis pavilions in the rear. The new sensitivity of McKim, Mead & White for an architecture of calmness, order and continuity of surface is evident in a comparison with Richard Morris Hunt's Traver's Block (1871) next door, with its restless agitation and fragmentation of parts. Sheldon described the Casino front as "an extremely beautiful adaptation of Early and Modern English."[4] The closest source was R. Norman Shaw's Hostelry and Stores in Bedford Park, though they were more vertical. On the Casino, McKim made a horizontal composition, three reiterated cross gables cap the long horizontal sweep of the floors. The voids of the ground level (framed in brick) contrast with the overhanging volumetric billowing of the shingled upper stories. Five different-shaped shingles catch the sun and create

74. *The Hostelry and 'The Stores,' Bedford Park, England, 1878. Richard Norman Shaw, architect; Maurice B. Adams, delineator.*

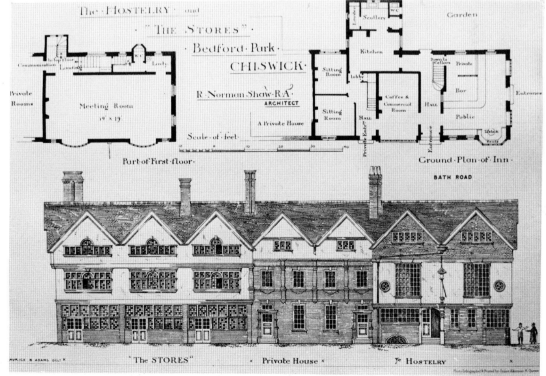

75. *Conversation room, ca. 1881*

76. *Theater. The interior is credited to White.*

an impressionistic display of light flickering across the surface. The wood reliefs in the gables and on the second floor, the cornice and frieze with sunflowers, the balustrade and the third-floor Palladian window are Queen Anne features. The bay window on the second floor shown in the drawing was replaced by a porch.

Passing through the entrance arch to the horseshoe court, the visitor entered a landscape composed of shingles, spindels and balustrades. The contrast of solid and void, of textured surfaces and dark cavities, created by the piazzas gave the sense of refuge from the glare of summertime sun. The interwoven balustrades and spindels treated as screens defined a horizontal spatial flow and luminescent boundary. The whimsical bell-shaped roof on the clock tower, the involved details, are evidence of White's more picturesque eye.

The Casino has experienced numerous alterations and rebuildings. McKim, Mead & White enclosed some of the piazzas and changed the interior in the early 1880s. Later, fire, hurricanes and changing uses took their toll. Still, the exterior is preserved remarkably well. The club rooms have been remodelled for the most part, though some of the original mantels in a variety of motifs can still be seen.

[1] George William Sheldon, *Artistic Country-Seats* (New York: D. Appleton & Co., 1886), vol. II: 101.

[2] Newport *Mercury*, August 30, 1879. See also, Richard O'Connor, *The Golden Summers* (New York: G. P. Putnam's & Sons, 1974), 103–05.

[3] Newport *Mercury*, October 25, 1879; November 7, 1879; December 6, 1879; and January 10, 1880.

[4] Sheldon, *Artistic Country-Seats*, vol. I: 68.

77. *Theater detail*

78. *Detail of mosaic on north wall*

## Samuel Tilton House
## 12 Sunnyside Place
## Newport, Rhode Island
## 1880–82

The Tilton house represents one of McKim, Mead & White's lower priced solutions to the summer cottage from the early 1880s. Originally projected as costing $9,000, it cost in excess of $16,000 when completed. Compactly massed under a large gable, the awkward appendage of the music room was probably added to the program after designs were nearly complete and accounted for the added cost. Exterior covering varies between the half timber and stucco on the north and west approach and shingles on the remainder. The mosaics in the stucco of shells, pebbles, glass and coal chips are semi-abstract representations of a sunburst and shield. Their origin lies in seventeenth-century New England prototypes. A relatively small

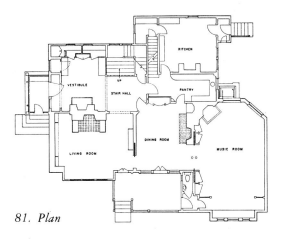

*81. Plan*

*79. Northwest view, ca. 1884*

*80. South elevation*

75

84. *Screen in vestibule*

82. *Vestibule and hall*

83. *Living room, north wall*

side hall serves as the organizing center for the major rooms, except for the poorly related music room. The hall is dominated by an elaborate fireplace of pale orange marble that contrasts with the dark wood and framed insets of spindles on the other walls. The paneling is seven feet high and topped by a prominent cornice sixteen inches below the ceiling that continues around the entire room. Highlights of brass hinges and escutcheons with brass brads add decorative touches. The parlor is more orthodox Queen Anne, with the built-in seats of a dark green color with gold highlights. The fireplace composition, using shell motifs reflects an American Colonial ancestry common to Newport.

85. *First-floor staircase*

86. *Entrance. The bay to the left is a later addition.*

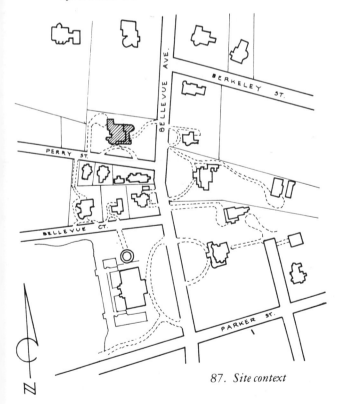

87. *Site context*

## Issac Bell, Jr., House
## "Edna Villa"
## 70 Perry Street
## Newport, Rhode Island
## 1881–83

An early announcement of the Bell house in the Newport papers claimed it would be a "Queen Anne villa"; this was followed in a few years with George W. Sheldon's description of it as "modernized colonial style"; and this was subsequently altered to the term "Shingle Style."[1] The confusion over what to call the Bell house indicates the difficulty of McKim, Mead & White's search for an American architectural image.

Located on the corner of Perry Street and Bellevue Avenue, the house actually faces on Bellevue, the major street, but the entrance is to the side. Sited well back on the small plot, lawn rolls up to the house, giving the impression of greater expanse. The area is the summer-house community but the house was actually constructed as a year-round dwelling. Issac Bell, Jr., was a New York cotton broker who married James Gordon Bennett's sister in 1878. Newport tradition holds that Bennett actually commissioned the house and gave it to his sister, but the McKim, Mead & White billbooks indicate Bell paid his own bills.[2] He moved permanently to Newport in 1883 and remained in the house until his death in 1889.[3] Samuel F. Barger, the Vanderbilt family lawyer, purchased the house in 1891 and gave it the name "Edna Villa."

88. Southeast view

Bell House

89. *Hall*

The composition of the house is dominated by the twin front gables that are voided at the base by the piazza which completely encircles the front. The projecting single-story portion balances the two-story composition on the other side. The base and the entire first floor are of red brick, and rubbed bricks are worked into quoins around openings and at corners. The mortar is red. Above this, shingles provide a textured contrast. The roof, originally shingled, provided a more emphatic roof plane. The side tower with the bell-shaped roof is perhaps a humorous reference to the owner's name. The porch posts are carved as large bamboo supports, and a further Oriental reference are twin carved Chinese dragons over the side entry.

The rotation of the house between front and entrance is further manifested in the plan, where the hall acts as the physical center which can be enclosed or opened as desired. The doors into the drawing room can be rolled back creating an opening sixteen feet wide and eight feet high, a significant diminishment of the wall plane. The windows in the outer wall of the drawing room and also the dining room are all cut to the floor and can be thrown open allowing passage outside to the piazza. While the spaces have the quality of being open to each other, still different interior decors preserve the particularity and individuality of each room. The drawing room was covered in white silk and had gold and white trim, whereas the hall was paneled in oak. The fireplace inglenook is set off with a dark stain and carved

90. *Hall, view toward drawing room*

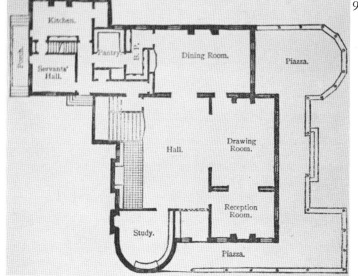

91. *Plan*

92. *Fireplace and overmantel detail*

with spindles and rosettes. The staircase, separated from the fireplace by a carved screen, has bottom risers eight feet wide at the bottom, which narrow to four feet at the landing. Bottle glass and light-color glass are used in the hall windows. Other rooms also received elaborate treatments; the dining room has a built-in buffet and several of the bedrooms have elaborate mantels.

Overall, the Bell house represents the creative interplay of the talents of the three partners in the early 1880s. None appears to have dominated the commission. The ellusive historical features of the design, while seen in a positive light many years later, proved troublesome at the same time, for Americans of the 1880s wanted a specificity of association not present in a modernized Colonial style.

[1] Newport *Mercury*, October 8, 1881, 1; George W. Sheldon, *Artistic Country Seats* (New York: D. Appleton & Co., 1886), vol. 1: 23; and Vincent J. Scully, Jr., *The Shingle Style and the Stick Style*, rev. ed. (New Haven: Yale University Press, 1971).

[2] Maud Howe Elliot, *This Was My Newport* (Cambridge, Mass.: Mythology Co., 1944), 161–62; and McKim, Mead & White Billbooks, The New-York Historical Society.

[3] Newport *Mercury*, January 26, 1889, 1.

93. *Staircase from first floor*

94. *Bedroom fireplace and mantel*

**Ross Winans House**
1217 St. Paul Street
Baltimore, Maryland
1882–83

This is a substantial city house with a large garden and fountain to the side and rear. The solidity of the front with the smooth-cut brownstone ashlar base and brick upper walls contrasts with the opening of the house to the rear. Multiple roof levels and a tower are tied together with horizontal bands and string courses to create a compact massing. Vertical accents are restrained. Nominally in the Francois I$^{er}$ style, with the flush laid-brownstone trim and decorative panels, Queen Anne sunbursts are worked in throughout. The particularized rooms on the first floor can open through sliding doors, forming various-sized compartments. The interiors are particularly fine and a variety of different mantels are still observable. McKim probably designed most of the exterior and White the interior. Cass Gilbert served as the firm's on-site superintendent and provided many details.

96. *Northwest view*

95. *Southwest view*

97. *Detail*

98. *Plan*

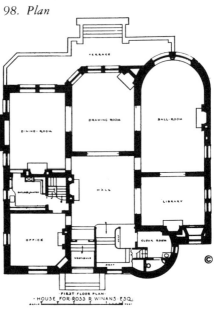

FIRST·FLOOR·PLAN·
·HOUSE·FOR·ROSS·R·WINANS·ESQ·

99. *Detail*

101. *Fireplace and mantel in ballroom*

100. *Fireplace and mantel in bedroom*

**Mrs. Frzelia Stetson Metcalfe House
Buffalo, New York
1882–84
Demolished**

The Metcalfe house represented an attempt by McKim, Mead & White to create a modernized Colonial suburban house, more substantive than the wooden resort cottage and free from the hallmarks of explicit revivalism. Russell Sturgis, writing in 1895, felt the house was one of "the less academical and more spontaneous . . . picturesque country buildings" of the firm.[1] The house was constructed out of red sandstone and brick, and terra-cotta tile shingles appeared in the gables and roof. A local magazine called the style "conventionalized 'early colonial,'" and "plain almost to homeliness, the long, steep pitch of its red-tiled roof suggesting ample provision made against the rigors of a northern winter."[2]

The side-hall plan was a variation on the one used for the Tilton house. Elaborate quartered oak carved in various geometrical patterns and broken by spindels, lattice and nitches covered the hall. The hall was conceived as a major living space and not simply a passageway. Marianna Griswold van Rensselaer, writing in 1886, claimed: "In our climate and with our social ways of summer-living, we absolutely require just what it [the hall] can give us—a room which in its uses shall stand midway between the piazzas on the one hand and the drawing-room and libraries on the other; perfectly

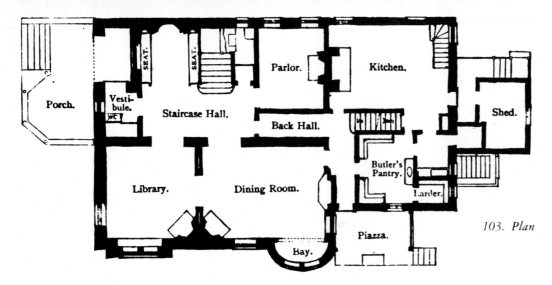

*103. Plan*

104. *Hall just prior to destruction. At some date the left-hand portion was altered.*

105. *Dining room*

106. *Bedroom*

107. *Bedroom*

*108. Staircase glass*

109. *Hall, detail of staircase spindle screen*

comfortable to live in when the hour means idleness, ease of access from all points outside and in, largely open to breeze and view, yet with generous hearthstone where we may find a rallying-point in days of cold and rain; in short, a spacious yet cozy and informal lounging-place for times when we cannot lounge on our beloved piazzas."[3]

Unfortunately the house was little appreciated by later-day critics and historians who could not shove it into one of their preconceived stylistic categories, and consequently it was wantonly demolished in 1979 for a parking lot. The elaborate interiors were dispersed to various museums and collectors; the hall will be erected as part of the period-room collection of the Metropolitan Museum of Art in New York.

[1] Russell Sturgis, "The Work of McKim, Mead & White," *Architectural Record*, Great American Architects Series (May, 1895): 71.

[2] "The Metcalfe Residence," *Buffalo Real Estate and Builder's Monthly* (January 1886), vol. II: 3.

[3] Marianna Griswold van Rensselaer, "American Country Dwellings, II," *Century* 32 (June 1886): 216.

110. *Hall, detail of frieze*

111. *Hall, view toward staircase*

*112. West view*

# MᶜKIM, MEAD & WHITE
## *Buildings of the Consolidation Period*

**Henry G. Villard Houses**
**451 Madison Avenue**
**New York, New York**
**1882–86**

Henry G. Villard must rank as one of McKim, Mead & White's most important patrons, for he commissioned not only the epoch-making Villard houses, but also he had them extensively remodel his country house in Dobb's Ferry, New York, and design stations and hotels for the Northern Pacific Railroad in Portland, Oregon and Tacoma, Washington.[1] In many ways, Villard typifies the shifting strains of American idealism in the post-Civil War years. Born in Germany he came to the United States in 1854 and became involved in the abolitionist movement as a newspaper reporter. He married Fanny Garrison, the daughter of William Lloyd Garrison, the great abolitionist. Charles McKim was related to the Garrisons through the marriage of a sister to one of Garrison's sons. In 1865 Villard helped found, with James Miller McKim and Frederick Law Olmsted, *The Nation* magazine. In the 1870s Villard turned to more materialistic pursuits and became in time a transportation czar of the Pacific Northwest with extensive interests in railroads, steamship companies and land. In 1882, feeling he had arrived, Villard approached his old friend Charles McKim for a house design to be located on a half city block on Madison Avenue in New York City.

The design for the Villard houses

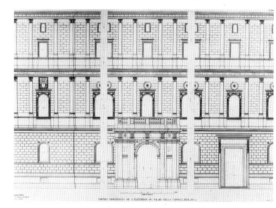

*113. Palazzo Cancelleria, Rome*

*114. Cancelleria courtyard*

95

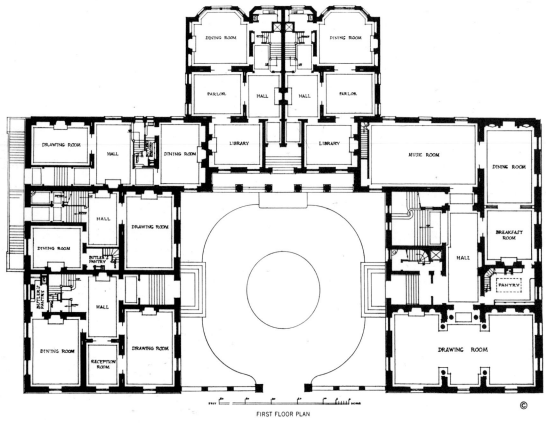

FIRST FLOOR PLAN

HENRY VILLARD, RESIDENCE, NEW YORK CITY.
1885

*115. Plan*

marked the first major appearance of Italian Renaissance precedent in the firm's design, though actually, McKim had used earlier some Italian Renaissance motives.[2] It marked the direction of the firm's work toward a more specific historical recall. The design responsibility was spread among the three partners and several draughtsmen, with Joseph Morrill Wells apparently reponsible for the facade design. Based upon the Palazzo Cancelleria in Rome, thought at the time to have been designed by Bramante, the details were simplified, the pilastration was eliminated and the window surrounds were reversed. The open courtyard did not follow the Cancelleria, though the precedent can be found in numerous European buildings—from the rear elevation of the Pitti Palazzo to the entrance to Versailles. The open courtyard in the New York palazzo was both an urban gesture to the fast-moving Madison Avenue traffic and a symbolic revelation of the occupant's wealth, in that such high-priced real estate could be left open. The symbolic value of the courtyard is revealed in the plans: Villard's house is not located on the major axis but on a cross axis, and two of the houses have entrances from a side street. Villard's scheme encompassed selling the individual houses to friends and various business associates. McKim, Mead and White were reponsible for most of the other houses, except one of the central houses, No. 483, whose owner thought the firm too expensive.[3]

The interior of Villard's house was the major focal point, and artistic friends of McKim, Mead & White's were invited

116. *Dining room*

*117. Entry-hall fireplace and overmantel. The sculptures have been attributed to Augustus Saint-Gaudens and the young Frederick MacMonnies.*

to collaborate on the designs. The rigor of the exterior gave way to a sensuous play of forms, colors and styles. The main hall, fourteen feet wide and forty-three feet long, had walls of Mexican marble, floors and vaulted ceilings of mosaic and was spanned by three arches. The dining room had a fireplace wall of Nubian marble containing three busts by Louis Saint-Gaudens and two fountain niches with carved fish by Augustus Saint-Gaudens.

Unfortunately for Mr. Villard his finances did not prosper and he had to vacate and sell the house shortly after completion. Recently, the houses have been converted into a forecourt and auxiliary structures for the Palace Hotel.[4]

[1] William C. Shopsin and Mosette Glaser Broderick, *The Villard Houses: Life Story of a Landmark* (New York: The Viking Press, 1980); Peter C. Neger, "American: The Villard Houses, 1882–85," *American Art Review* III (September–October 1976): 119–28; and Henry Villard, *Memoirs of Henry Villard* (New York and Boston: Houghton Mifflin & Co., 1904), 2 vols.

[2] Of the several designs prior to the Villard houses utilizing Italian Renaissance precedent, McKim, Mead & Bigelow's, Union League Club competition entry of 1879 is the most important and draws directly upon the Villa Medici. McKim was given credit for the design. See, *American Architect and Building News,* 5 (June 7, 1879): 180, and (April 4, 1879): 133–34.

[3] Letter, Artemas H. Holmes to McKim, Mead & White, January 5, 1885, The New-York Historical Society.

[4] On the conversion see, Shopsin and Broderick, *The Villard Houses*; James W. Rhodes, "Preservation of the Villard Houses"; and William T. Weber, "Restoring the Landmark Interiors . . . ," *Technology and Conservation* 5 (Winter 1980): 32–37 and 38–46.

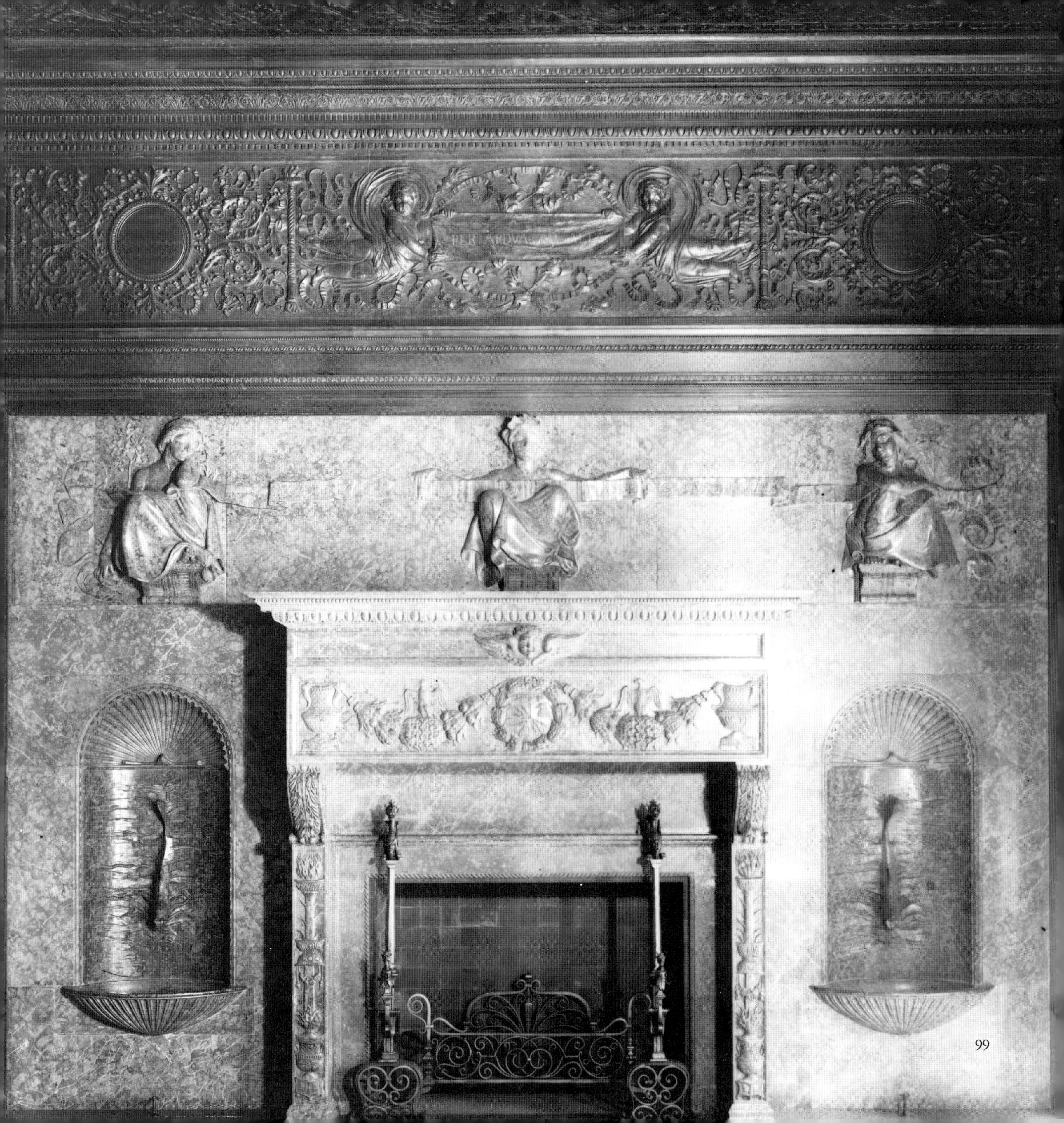
PER ARDUA

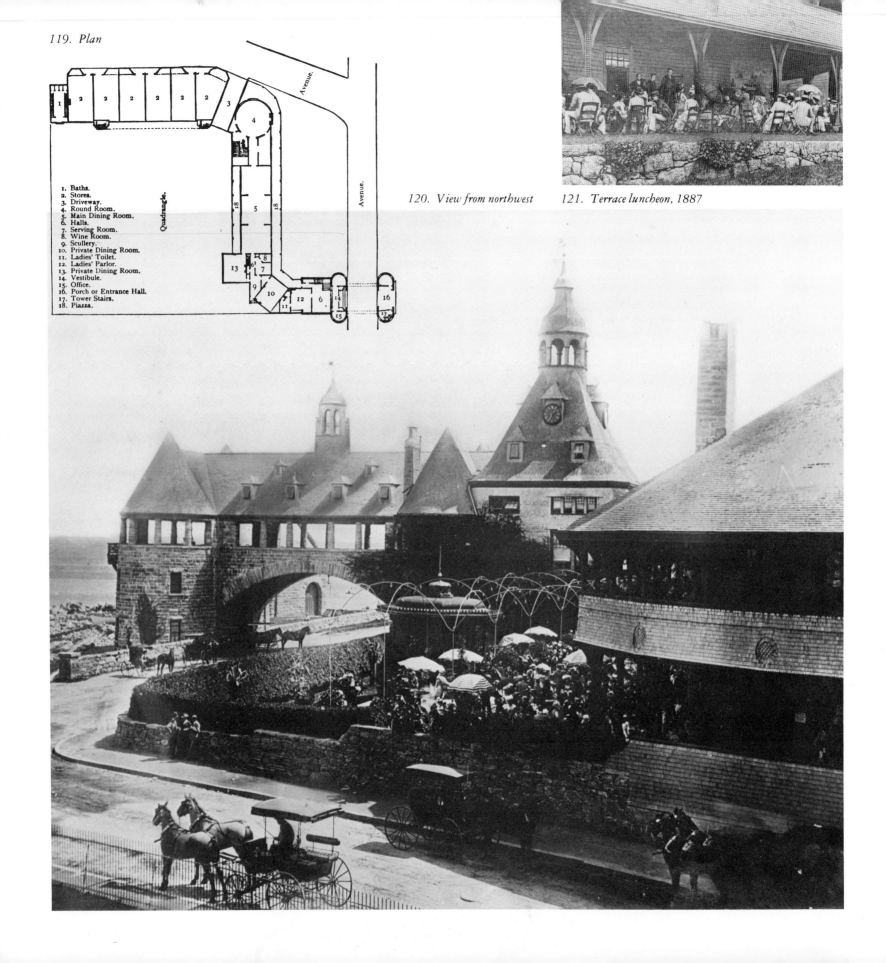

119. *Plan*

1. Baths.
2. Stores.
3. Driveway.
4. Round Room.
5. Main Dining Room.
6. Halls.
7. Serving Room.
8. Wine Room.
9. Scullery.
10. Private Dining Room.
11. Ladies' Toilet.
12. Ladies' Parlor.
13. Private Dining Room.
14. Vestibule.
15. Office.
16. Porch or Entrance Hall.
17. Tower Stairs.
18. Piazza.

120. *View from northwest*    121. *Terrace luncheon, 1887*

**Narragansett Pier Casino
Narragansett, Rhode Island
1883–86
Partially Demolished**

*122. View from southeast*

The Narragansett Pier Casino, commissioned in 1883, was a direct reflection of the success of the Newport Casino. A writer for *Harper's Weekly* summed up Narragansett Pier: "The habitues of the place are, in general, people of the same social standing as those of Newport, and have in the main less money."[1] The Casino Company had on its board of directors George V. Cresson and Rowland G. Hazard, both of whom McKim, Mead & White were to do houses for, as well as Dr. Charles Hitchcock, McKim's New York physician. Louis Sherry, the New York restaurateur, ran the restaurant in the casino for many years. Later, McKim, Mead & White would do another building for him in Narragansett. Frederick Law Olmsted designed the landscaping.[2]

The Narragansett Pier Casino provides an instructive contrast with the Newport Casino, indicating the tendency towards greater monumentality and heaviness. Rising only a few feet from the water's edge were high, rough-faced ashlar towers that carried the fifty-foot arch spanning the roadway. The origin of the arch lay with the towers of the Loire Valley and European city gates. Piled on top of the dark void of an open-air cafe were high pitched roofs carrying dormers, belfries and lookouts. The roofs were described by a *Harper's Weekly* corres-

pondent as "irregularly rounded and dented to suggest the effect of ravaging winds."[3] Reportedly at the completion of construction, McKim had climbed out on the roof and pried up some of the shingles to further the effect of wear.[4] The impact was one of age, of a battered structure that had withstood the forces of nature and man.

The archway, in spite of its appearance, acted as an appendange to the main portion of the casino, a long wooden structure which swept out to the side in the Olmsted grounds. On several levels were stores, dining rooms and cafes, a billiard room, a theater and lounge rooms. Informally accessible from a variety of points, piazzas opened off nearly all levels and created dark ribbons of flow-

ing space, contrasting with the textured shingles and rough stone. The wooden portions and the roof of the casino were destroyed by fire in the early 1900s, and rebuilt with a small appendage to the tower by J. Howard Adams of Providence. In 1938, it was again damaged. Today the towers and arch remain, a romantic ruin, a remembrance of the past that would have pleased McKim.

[1] "Narragansett and its Casino," *Harper's Weekly* 31 (August 27, 1887): 611.

[2] Frederick Law Olmsted, Jr. and Theodora Kimball, eds., *Frederick Law Olmsted, Landscape Architect, 1822–1903* (New York: Benjamin Blom, 1970), vol. 1: 27; and Letter, William R. Mead to Frederick Law Olmsted, March 20, 1885, Library of Congress, Washington, D.C.

[3] "Narragansett," *Harper's Weekly*, 611.

[4] Charles H. Reilly, *McKim, Mead & White* (London: Ernest Benn, Ltd., 1924), 20.

123. *Front elevation. Ink on linen.*

124. *Front elevation as built*

## Le Roy King House
## Berkeley and Bellevue Avenues
## Newport, Rhode Island
## 1884–86

The Le Roy King commission came to the McKim, Mead & White offices in April 1884, and by November 22, 1884, plans were completed and ground was broken. The builder was William J. Underwood. The house was completed in 1886 at a cost of about $10,000. Family tradition gives Stanford White credit as the designer since he had been working for Le Roy King's brother, David King, Jr., on "Kingscote," a short distance up Bellevue Avenue. At this point in the life of the McKim firm, it is doubtful if any partner had total control of a project, rather the King house is representative of a transition the firm was going through and is contemporaneous with the Commodore William G. Edgar house. The plan is tightly controlled, with a through center hall similar to the Edgar and Choate designs. Rooms and staircase open off the hall.

More self-contained than earlier Newport resort houses by the firm, the King house is more urban; sited at the lot's edge and with virtually no setback from the street, it marks a departure from other Bellevue Avenue houses. The entry is from Berkeley and not Bellevue Avenue. The facades are balanced with nearly identical end pavilions topped by prominent gables. The entrance is off center, but balanced by the stair tower; on the rear, a balance is achieved

125. *Rear elevation. Ink on linen.*

126. *Rear elevation as built*

127. *Newel post, based upon 18th century Newport examples*

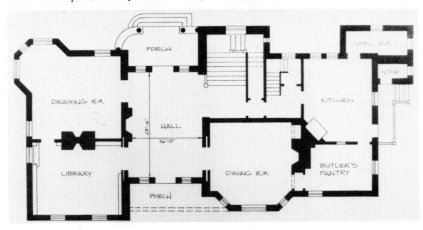

128. *Plan*

between the garden entrance and the dining-room window. As projected in the drawings, the house, with the exception of the stair tower, was to have been largely covered in shingles. As built, red brick is used for the two main floors and random ashlar for the rough granite stair tower. Shingles do appear in the garden facade gables, while the front gables are covered in pebble dash. The change in materials makes the house even more urban in character and recalls the red-brick Queen Anne along the Chelsea embankment in London. The overall monochromatic use and the appearance of Colonial details, such as the Palladian windows in the front gables, and the stair tower windows, all indicate the increasingly classical orientation of the firm. Faintly sketched on the front elevation was a widow's walk that was included on the completed house.

Interior woodwork is particularly fine. The staircase newel posts are reinterpretations of eighteenth-century Newport examples that McKim had photographed in 1874–75. In the early-twentieth century, Frederick Rhinelander King made an extension to the house. Today the house exists in excellent condition.

129. *Staircase hall*

*130. Rear, south view*

Commodore William G. Edgar House
29 Old Beach Road
Newport, Rhode Island
1884–86

131. *Front, northwest view*

The Commodore William G. Edgar house, along with the nearly contemporaneous houses by McKim, Mead & White—the H. A. C. Taylor house, Newport (1883–85, now destroyed) and the Misses Appleton house, Lenox (1883–84, also destroyed)—indicate the direction of American architecture in the mid-1880s towards greater formality, control and historical recall. Possibly the first American Georgian Revival house constructed of brick, the Edgar house demonstrates how McKim, Mead & White typically departed rather liberally from the original prototypes. George William Sheldon, writing in 1886, claimed: "Although disclosing some affinity with the colonial style, this house can scarcely be classed as colonial."[1]

The rendering, probably by Stanford White, with its soft focus and dreamy childlike air, conveys a nostalgia akin to the English Queen Anne. Consequently, while the form and many details are American, the handling is reminiscent of contemporary work by Richard Norman Shaw and Philip Webb. Also, the brick is not an imitation of eighteenth-century red brick, but a long, narrow and buff-colored Roman type, of which McKim, Mead & White were especially

132. *Plan*

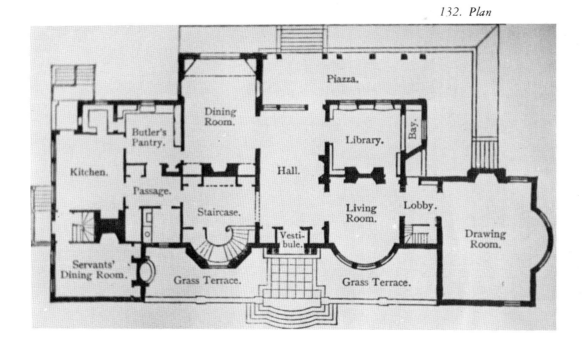

133. *Front door from interior. The form is obviously a witty play upon Commodore Edgar's naval career.*

134. *Stairhall*

135. *Hall*

## Edgar House

fond and made popular. Onto the overall form, which recalls southern mansions, details are collaged: chimneys from Stratford Hall or Independence Hall, a widow's walk from Salem or Newport and a portico from Bulfinch's Beacon Hill. Between the rendering and the completed house, changes were made—some of the white trim was toned down and eliminated, and a second-floor piazza was inserted in the right wing.

In spite of the monumental facade, the interior with its low ceilings has a feeling of intimacy. The plan contains a straight-through hall with surrounding spaces treated as discrete volumes. The hall measures 20 feet by 16½ feet, and has a rear wall of glass that during the day gives the appearance of being open. Dark oak and simulated leather covered the hall's walls; a large French medieval mantel dominated the center of one wall. Other interior decoration is particularly fine: the dining room contains a complete wall of glass cabinets surrounding the fireplace, the stairhall is Adamesque with brass balusters and a velvet covered rail, and the ballroom has a ceiling mural possibly by Thomas Dewing or Frances Lathrop. Overall, the house is typical of the close collaboration between McKim, Mead & White during the 1880s. In 1885, *The Art Age* ascribed the design to White. He replied in a letter: "No member of our firm is ever individually responsible for any design which goes out from it."[2]

[1] George William Sheldon, *Artistic Country-Seats* (New York: D. Appleton & Co., 1886), vol. II: 25.

[2] *The Art Age* 3 (January 1886): 100; see also, (December 1885): 86–87.

136. *Dining room with built-in cabinets. Local tradition claims White imported the ceiling from Europe.*

137. *Library*

138. *Chateau de Martainville, ca. 1485*

## Mrs. Mark Hopkins House
## Great Barrington, Massachusetts
## ca. 1884–86

The Hopkins house was the first truly lavish country mansion that the firm designed, a building type that would extensively occupy them in later years. Estimates of its cost were published as high as $5 million.[1] A figure of $500,000 is probably more correct, at least as an initial estimate. The widow of one of the members of California railroads' "Big 4," Mary Sherwood Hopkins returned to her hometown and embarked on a large building campaign with Stanford White as chief designer. Construction began in April 1885, and in January 1886, after the basic shell of the house had been erected, the firm was discharged on construction contracts of $200,000.[2] White was replaced by Edward F. Searles, an interior decorator reputedly with Herter Brothers. Searles was twenty-one years Mrs. Hopkins's junior, but that hardly prevented him from becoming her husband in 1887. She died in 1891 and he inherited most of her wealth.[3] Searles designed most of the interior decor—which has been altered over the years—but the plan and exterior are by McKim, Mead & White.

Baronial in evocation, this house drew upon the Loire Valley chateaux that White knew from his 1878 trip. He may also have drawn upon images printed in Claude Sauvageot's *Palais, Châteaux & Hotels* (1867), a standard architectural tome in most offices of the time.[4] The

139. *Garden elevation*

140. Front

stone, a local blue dolomite, has a Richardsonian toughness. Sited well back from the road and surrounded by a high fence, the house is best seen from a meadow that runs across the rear, where the composition of turrets, towers and spires begins to resemble an old world chateau. On the main entrance front the loggia, more Italian Renaissance in style, was apparently derived from the Villa Medici. The contrast between the seemingly picturesque form and the highly controlled plan with the alignment of the three atriums—the reception vestibule, the main hall and the exterior covered terrace—was typical of McKim, Mead & White's work from the Consolidation Period of the mid-1880s, when the plan was beginning to dominate and provide an order.

[1] Clippings from the *Berkshire Courier,* February 23, 1885, April 22, 1885; *Chicago Building Budget,* April, 1885; and others in the *McKim, Mead & White Scrapbook,* The New-York Historical Society. See also, Charles Baldwin, *Stanford White* (New York: Dodd, Mead & Co., 1931), 177.

[2] *McKim, Mead & White Billbooks,* The New-York Historical Society.

[3] Charles J. Taylor, *History of Great Barrington (Berkshire) Massachusetts* (Great Barrington: Town of Great Barrington, 1928), 478–80.

[4] Henry-Russell Hitchcock, *The Architecture of H. H. Richardson and His Times* rev. ed., (Cambridge: MIT Press, 1966), 102.

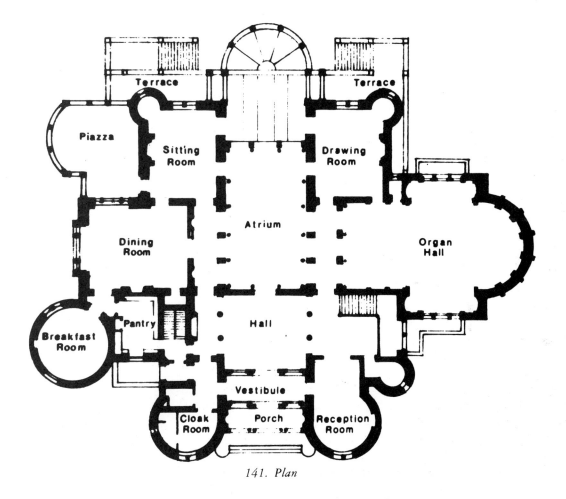

*141. Plan*

*142. Northwest view*

## Joseph H. Choate House
## "Naumkeag"
## Stockbridge, Massachusetts
## 1884–87

Designed for Joseph H. Choate, a prominent and wealthy lawyer who successfully argued the unconstitutionality of the income tax in 1894 to the Supreme Court and later ambassador to Great Britain, the house is sited on a prominent ridge overlooking the town. Frederick Law Olmsted originally sited the house halfway down the hillside, but Charles McKim, feeling the more commanding site was important, had Olmsted dismissed and called in another landscape architect, Nathan Barrett. Stanford White was primarily responsible for the design which represented a movement away from the modernized Colonial and a search for greater antiquity, or as one local commentator claimed, it was "somewhat in the Old English style."[1]

A picturesque approach was assembled composed of the high roof, dormers, porte cochère and tower, and assisted by the rubble stone, the glass slag in the cement and the irregular stone quoins. In contrast, the rear or terrace side is wooden and dominated by the twin-shingled gables. The plan is neatly func-

143. *Southeast view*

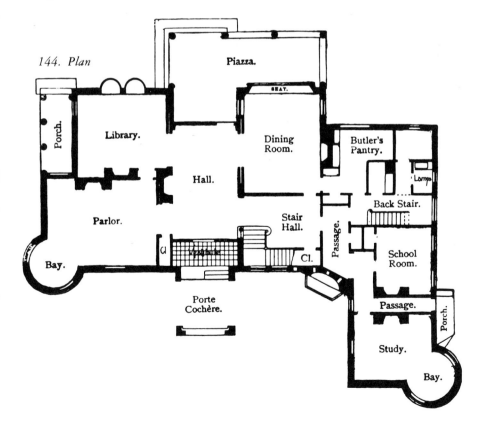

144. *Plan*

145. *Parlor, ca. 1900*

146. *Dining room, ca. 1900*

## Choate House

tional and yet formal. A transverse hall bisects the main public spaces into four nearly equal particulated spaces, Choate's private study is removed, and the service areas, integrated into the mass for formal effect, are completely subsidiary. The interior is one of the best preserved houses from the period and combines aesthetic movement originality with more exact replicas, as in the hall fireplace hood.

[1] *Berkshire Courier,* October 27, 1886.

147. *Dining room, mantel detail*

148. *Hall*

149. *Stairhall*

150.  *Northwest, waterside view, 1962*

## William Gilman Low House
## Bristol, Rhode Island
## 1886–87
## Demolished

The pressures of running a large, far-flung architecture practice were outlined in a note White sent to McKim in 1886: "By the way I want you to arrange—if you can—to go on to Bristol—near Providence—with a Mr. Low Wednesday night of next week about a house. I have to be in Baltimore and it is the only time he can go—he is a strange but a bully fellow."[1]

Sited overlooking Narragansett Bay in Bristol, a summer community lacking the pretensions and wealth of nearby Newport, the Low house cost $12,082.40, plus architect's commission of 5 percent. William G. Low was a New York lawyer with a home in Brooklyn. His brother was Seth Low, the mayor of Brooklyn, and the instigator of the Soldiers' and Sailors' Arch, later the president of Columbia University and instrumental in McKim's gaining the campus commission, and still later the mayor of New York.

In the Low house McKim gathered all the elements of the house and submerged them under a great triangular gable or pediment. The roof was the house. Slight eruptions occurred with the twin bulging bays on the bay side, and the deep penetration of the porch but overall the predetermined form was paramount. Straight-cut cypress shingles covered the

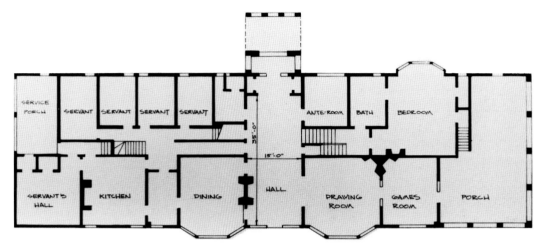

151. First-floor plan

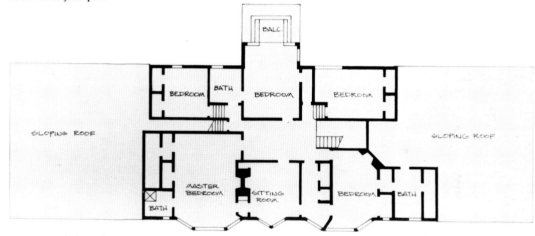

152. Second-floor plan

119

153. *Southwest, waterside view, 1962*

*154. Southeast, landside view, 1962*

## Low House

*155. Second-floor sitting room*

*156. Staircase*

exterior surfaces, other trim was confined to thin moldings.

The problems of the dominant form were apparent in the eccentric fenestration patterns and the plan, where six different interior levels were used. A straight-through living hall divided the house on the ground floor in one direction, and cross-axial corridors separated it in the other. Interior trim was minimal—some turned balustrades and moldings for doors and mantels.

The Low house has become known as one of McKim, Mead & White's most original designs. In a sense it marked the culmination of McKim's experimentation with the large gable form in the Butler and Howells houses. He evidently saw the Low design as somewhat problematical, or as a "fancy," and when William Low demurred at the extreme geometrical character, McKim persuaded him to go on and have it built.[2] In a sense the design marked his last fling with the modernized Colonial style, and thereafter he and his partners would turn to more recognizable historical models. The house was demolished in the early 1960s by a new owner as uneconomical and replaced by a Cape Cod bungalow.

[1] Letter, White to McKim, undated (ca. September 1886), New York Public Library.

[2] Author interview with Mrs. A. Little (daughter of William Low), July 21, 1977. Mrs. Little confirmed that McKim was the architect.

157. *Hall, view toward front door*

158. *Second-floor hall*

**George Sealy House**
**2424 Broadway**
**Galveston, Texas**
**1886–91**

The George Sealy house is one of the few McKim, Mead & White residences west of the Mississippi River and their only building in Texas. It indicates their attempt to respond to the semi-tropical local environment and the perceived lack of a local tradition. Galveston is located on a flat, sandy island which is frequently swept by hurricanes and tidal waves. Hence, the house follows local tradition and is placed high off the ground. It was the first house in Galveston to have a working cellar. The plan is a variation on the tightly controlled central-hall schemes typical in their work during this period. The large piazzas off the major rooms and the fenestration placement indicates some attempt to recognize the problem of hot summers.

How the Sealys, a local banking family, discovered McKim, Mead & White is uncertain. In 1885 the firm began work on designs for a house with a local architect, Nicholas Clayton. Family tradition, however, assigns the house to Stanford White. By January 1887, Clayton's diary records correspondence with the firm, who furnished drawings and samples of building materials and trim, while Clayton acted as the local representative and later designed the carriage house on the property in the same style.[1] Whether any member of the firm ever visited Galveston is unknown, but doubtful.

While the forms such as the tower re-

semble earlier houses such as the Bell house, the overall intent appears to have been to create a Mediterranean style of building. Light-colored Roman brick, the red-tile roof and the arches were White's attempt to create a style harmonious with the environment. Onto this were grafted certain classical details, the terra-cotta swag frieze, the Tuscan columns on the second-floor piazza and the antifixae ends of the roof tiles.

The interior is a particularly lush example of the firm's work. The hall is of dark American quartered oak. A Renaissance-styled arch separates the staircase from the reception area. The drawing room and music niche were to be in enameled white with gold trim. However, in 1915 these rooms were remodeled by Elsie de Wolfe. The dining room has wainscoting and trim in Honduras mahogany, and the upper walls are covered in a red fibrine or canvas, studded with brass tacks in a delicate classical pattern.

162. *Hall*

¹ The assistance of Drexel Turner of Rice University and the expert on Nicholas Clayton is gratefully acknowledged. He and Stephan Fox have furnished me with much information. See also, Clayton's letter to the editors, *American Architect and Building News* 22 (October 1, 1887): 163; Drury Blake Alexander, *Texas Homes of the Nineteenth Century* (Austin: University of Texas Press, 1966), 231–32; and Elizabeth Gustafson, "The Open Gates, The George Sealy House in Galveston," *Antiques* CVIII (September, 1975): 508–14.

163. *Plan*

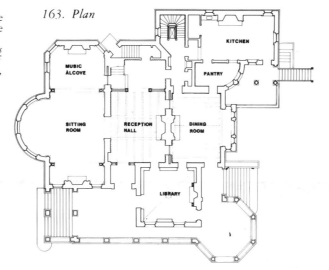

164. *Study for exterior front. Watercolor, ink and pencil rendering.*

165. *Study for exterior front. Pencil and ink on paper.*

## Rowland Gibson Hazard House
## "Holly House"
### Peacedale, Rhode Island
### 1891–93
### Demolished

Rowland Gibson Hazard III (1855–1918) was one of McKim, Mead & White's more important patrons, serving on the board of directors of the Narragansett Pier Casino and as a member of the new Rhode Island State House Commission. He was an industrialist and ran the family business, the Peacedale Manufacturing Company, and also served as vice president of the Solvay Process Company of Syracuse, New York.

Hazard first became acquainted with McKim, Mead & White through the Narragansett Pier Casino, and in 1886 they designed a house for him which was never constructed and the plans were lost. In October 1891, he contacted Charles McKim about making alterations to the house of his recently deceased father, a ca. 1855 stone, Gothic-style cottage. By October 23, McKim had supplied initial plans and explained that the intention was to "build a new house of the same size as the old one, thus gaining a balanced scheme and representing as nearly as possible the room called for in your program."[1] The initial plans underwent considerable revision in the next nine months as revealed in Hazard's diary: "Nov. 13 [1891] N.Y. To see McKim. Saw Holyoke. May 2nd [1892] Plans of house in total confusion."[2] The design took place concur-

STUDY OF ENTRANCE · HOUSE FOR R.G. HAZARD ESQ.
McKim Mead & White Arch't's        Peace Dale R.I.
1 W. 20th Street. New York.

*167. Front*

*168. Rear*

*169. Hall, view toward dining room*

rently with the awarding of the Rhode Island State House commission to McKim, Mead & White. Construction began in May 1892, and the renamed "Holly House" was occupied in June 1893.

McKim was the partner-in-charge of the design, though Hazard's diary reveals that both Mead and an employee, Thomas G. Holyoke, who did some of the drawings, were responsible for many of the details. The drawings for Holly House are unique, being one of the most complete sets of McKim, Mead & White presentation drawings that have survived.

Formally, Holly House indicates the evolution of McKim, Mead & White's designs from the rambling wooden houses of the 1870s and early 1880s to a closed composition, balanced and reserved. Stylistically, the house was unique and recalled Elizabethan and Jacobean country houses in massing, fenestration and ornament. Restricted by the pre-existing stone house, McKim attempted other stylistic solutions as the two drawings which show alternative entrances, a colonnade and a Palladian doorway, indicate. The final solution was not an archaeological copy of any specific English house, but a simplification and creative adaptation. In contrast to the front, the rear had a more relaxed appearance, and a double porch in the Colonial style opened off one of the wings.

In plan, the left portion is the pre-existing house, with the original entrance now the "porch" and the "children's hall." How much McKim changed this

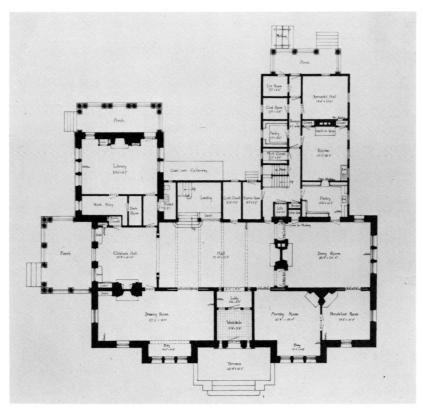

170. *Ground-floor plan*

171. *Second-floor plan*

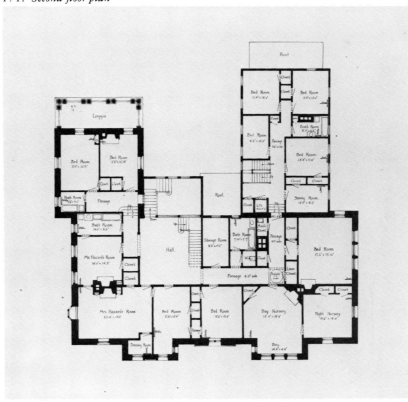

172. *Study for dining-room mantel. Ink on tracing paper signed "T. G. H., November 11, 1892."*

173. *Study for children's hall. Watercolor, pencil, ink on paper.*

*174. Design for library mantel. Ink and wash on tracing paper.*

·ELEVATION·

PLAN.     Scale ¾" per Foot.

·DESIGN FOR LIBRARY MANTEL· HOUSE FOR R.G.HAZARD ESQ· PEACE DALE.R.I.·

McKim Mead & White Archts ~ 1 W. 20 ~ New York.

configuration is unknown. The program requirement for more formal living spaces and service areas was apparent in the new section. The large hall dominated the house, spreading out horizontally, and vertically as well, through the staircase containing a large landing with built-in seats. In spite of the open hall, the interior decoration made each room a particularized unit. A variety of periods was repeated throughout. The children's hall was done in a semi-medieval, "Olde English" manner, communicated in the drawing by colors, motifs and the child's clothing. The library was Georgian and the parlor Adamesque. Irving & Casson Company of Boston provided many of the interiors and the furniture.

The house was demolished about 1952.

[1]  Letter, Charles F. McKim to Rowland Hazard, October 23, 1891, Library of Congress.

[2]  Diary of Rowland Gibson Hazard, Collection of Wallace Campbell, Wakefield, Rhode Island. See also, Catherine Hazard, ed., *Letters of Rowland Gibson Hazard* (Boston: D. B. Updike, 1922).

175. *Proposal of early scheme with four individual statues at the entrance, 1888*

**Boston Public Library**
**Copley Square**
**Boston, Massachusetts**
**1887–95**

The centerpiece of McKim, Mead & White's architecture, the Boston Public Library, was a major procreating force of the American Renaissance. The library was the first public building that demonstrated the possibilities of collaborative art, and was the first great example of "civic art." It was both democratic with its inscriptions—"Built by the People of Boston" and "Open to All"—and also aristocratic, with its elaborate decorative program. Located across from Henry Hobson Richardson's Trinity Church, upon which both McKim and White had worked, the building took on an Oedipal cast, for McKim and White symbolically disowned Richardson's stylistic solution and instead embraced classicism. The library pulled Boston out of the "Brown Decades" and brought it to the forefront of the light-colored years of the turn of the century.

McKim, Mead & White received the commission without competition in early 1887 after the library trustees had aborted a weak imitative Richardson Romanesque design by the Boston city architect, Arthur Vinal. Charles McKim was the partner-in-charge and together with Samuel A. B. Abbott, the president of the Board of Trustees, envisioned the building as a grand public-spirited Medician gesture, an attempt to raise the quality of the arts in America. Mod-

176. *Northeast view, ca. 1901. The Bella Pratt statues are not in place.*

**Boston Public Library**

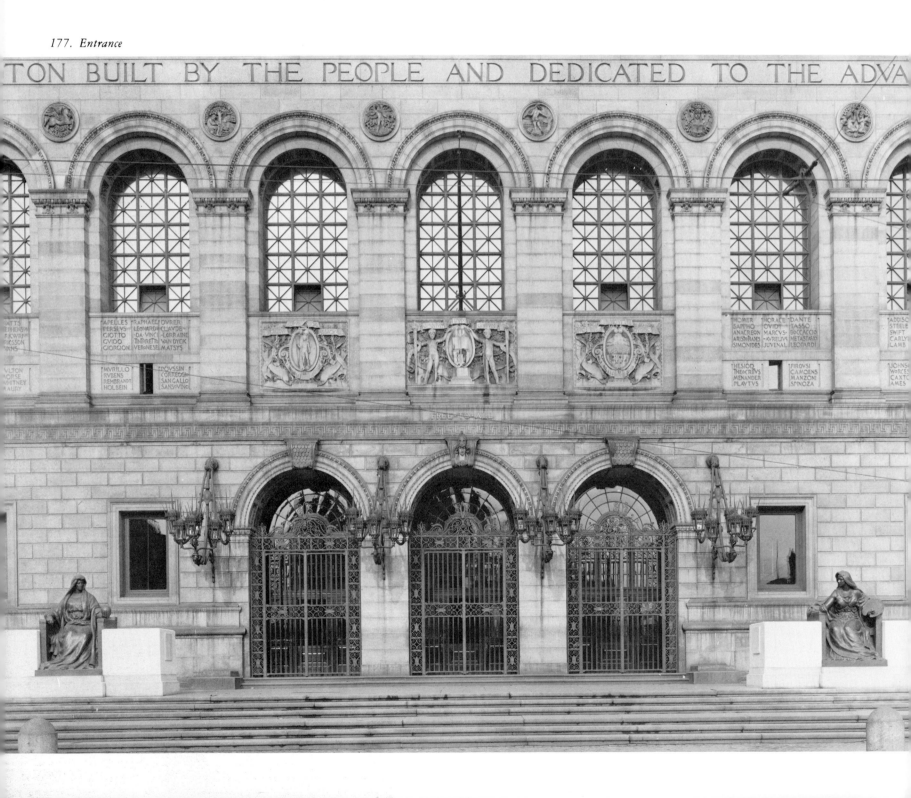

177. *Entrance*

178. *Entrance*

eled in the form of a freestanding Italian Renaissance palazzo, the building also had origins in Henri Labrouste's Bibliotheque Sainte Geneviève, Paris, and Alberti's Tempio Malatestiano, Rimini. The Paris library provided the organization for the front facade, the large *piano noble* reading room and the entry sequence. McKim has shortened the long arcade of the Labrouste building to thirteen arches, thereby confining the building into a more separate entity. The depth and detailing of McKim's arches recalled Alberti's Tempio. An early scheme for the building showed a single entrance arch rather than the triple portal as built, and also round-headed basement windows instead of square. McKim's concern over the exterior detailing went so far that he erected a trial section of cornice in order to check the shadow line details.

Into the preconceived courtyard plan, McKim forced the functional elements of the library. Naturally public and communication spaces received first priority, and an examination of the south-side elevation showed the insertion of more programmatic elements. The elaborate sequence of entry—vestibule, entry hall, stair hall—was terminated

179. *Erection of trial, plaster cornice*

180. Piano noble *and cornice detail*

*181. Main staircase with murals by Puvis de Chavannes and sculptures by Louis Saint-Gaudens*

awkwardly by a small door into Bates Hall, the grand public room. An early perspective of Bates Hall, without furniture but with pedestrians admiring the murals and the architecture, indicated the essentially ritualistic nature McKim saw for the building. The courtyard arcade was based upon the Cancelleria in Rome. (The sharp and flat drawing style used for several of the early perspectives was similar to that shown in Letarouily, *Edfices de Rome Moderne,* 1840–57, and indicated the continued reliance upon this source.) The courtyard with its arcade and fountain was an island of calm, a fragment of Rome within Boston. The building is basically a masonry structure of pink Milford granite with interior supports of cast iron and steel; Guastavino vaulting is used throughout.

From the beginning, McKim and Abbott intended the library to show the possibilities of decorative public art. Augustus Saint-Gaudens was to provide sculptural groups for the entrance, but having left them unfinished at his death, Bela Pratt contributed the figures of *Art* and *Science.* Saint-Gaudens did carve the three panels over the central door—the Seals of the City, State and the Library (the latter designed by Kenyon Cox in conjunction with Domingo Mora. They also contributed the head of *Minerva,* goddess of wisdom, in the keystone of the central arch. Mora did the medallions in the arch spandrels that represent printer's and bookseller's devices). The main bronze doors are by Daniel Chester French, and inside the vestibule stands a statue by Frederick MacMonnies is of

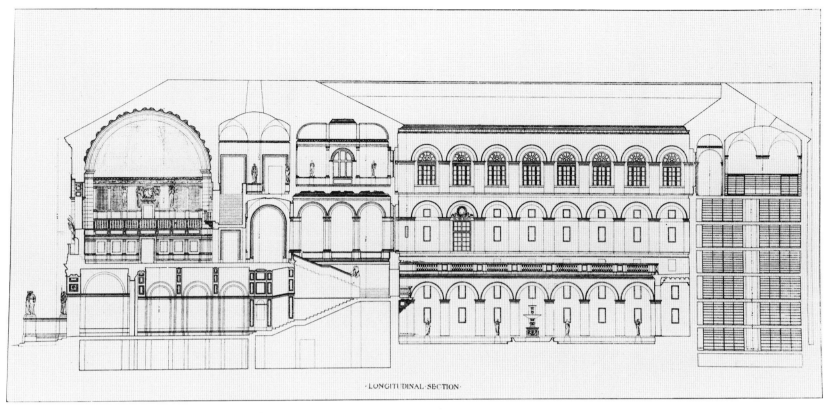

·LONGITUDINAL·SECTION·

182. *Longitudinal section, 1888. Note the differing treatments for statuary at front, Bates Hall, third-floor hall and courtyard.*

183. *Plans*

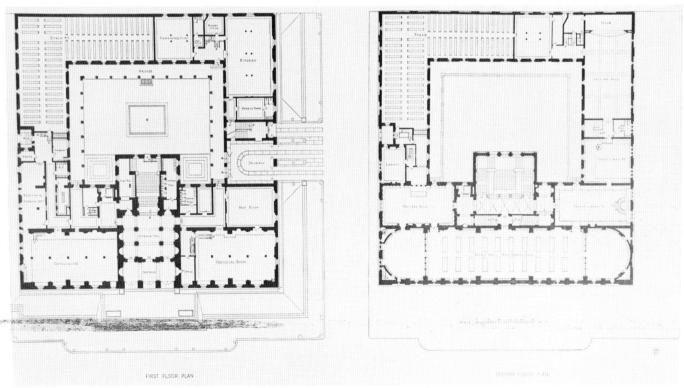

FIRST FLOOR PLAN

184. *Courtyard scheme, 1888*

186. *Palazzo Cancelleria courtyard*

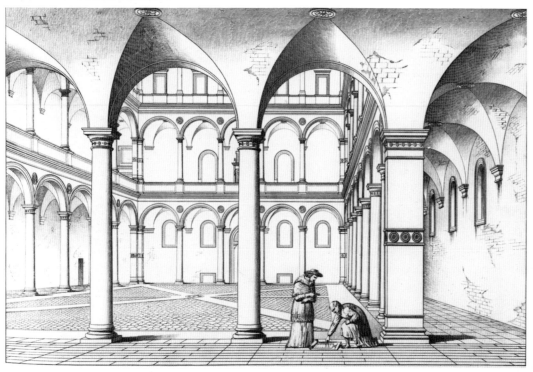

185. *Study for west gallery, 1888*

Sir Henry Vane, an early governor of the Massachusetts Bay Colony. In the staircase the lions, memorials to Massachusetts regiments of the Civil War, are by Louis Saint-Gaudens.

The stair-hall murals by Pierre Puvis de Chavannes are in a neo-Grec style representing *The Muses of Inspiration Hail the Spirit of Light and the Learned Disciplines*. Twin alcoves at either end are decorated in the Venetian style by Joseph Linden Smith and the Pompeian style by Elmer E. Garnsey. The Delivery Room contained murals by Edwin Austin Abbey, *Quest and Achievement of the Holy Grail*, and is paneled in dark oak and rouge antique marble. The Patent Room on the same floor has a mural, *The Triumph of Time*, by John Eliott. The third-floor hall is decorated by an extensive sequence of murals by John Singer Sargent on *Judaism and Christianity*. Through-

187. *Courtyard, ca. 1901*

188. *Study for Bates Hall, view to north, 1888*

*189. Bates Hall as completed, view to south. McKim selected the Windsor chairs.*

190. *Courtyard*

out the remainder of the building smaller decorative works were installed. The main reading room, Bates Hall, never received its intended mural. Called the "veritable Assisi of American Art,"[2] the library gives ample indication of aspirations for history and culture sought by McKim and his patrons.

The library was occupied in 1895, however the decorative work continued until 1916 when the last of Sargent's murals was installed. In 1964 Philip Johnson was commissioned to design an annex which was opened in 1973. The McKim building was designated as the Research Library and in the ensuing years some restoration has taken place. It still exists in good condition.

[1] On the history see: Walter Muir Whitehill, *The Boston Public Library: A Centennial History* (Cambridge: Harvard University Press, 1956); Whitehill, "The Making of an Architectural Masterpiece," *American Art Journal* 2 (Fall 1970): 13–35; and William Jordy, *American Buildings and Their Architects: Progressive and Academic Ideals at the Turn-of-the-Twentieth Century* (New York, 1972), vol. 3, ch. 7.

[2] Ernest Francisco Fenollosa, *Mural Painting in the Boston Public Library* (Boston: Curtis and Co., 1896), 25. See also, Henry James, *The American Scene* (New York and London: Harper and Brothers, 1907).

191. *Periodical reading room. Guastavino vaulting is visible in the ceiling.*

192. *Delivery room with Abbey murals*

193. *Northeast view across Washington Square, 1905*

**Judson Memorial Church
Tower and Hall
Washington Square South at
Thompson Street
New York, New York
1888–96**

While McKim, Mead & White were
never primarily known as ecclesiastical
architects, they made significant contri-
butions and helped reorient American
religious architecture away from the
Gothic and towards the classical and
Colonial past. The Judson borrowed
forms and details, from Italian Romanesque and Renaissance churches though
as usual they were transformed. As
the partner-in-charge, Stanford White
created a color spectacle with tan and
yellow Roman brick and terra cotta.
Characteristically, a wealth of ornament
covers the building. The basement floor,
with the deep rustication and guilloche-
patterned terra cotta, ties together the
different portions of the complex. The
church, a simple rectangular basilica,
stands one level above the street and is
articulated by arcades at the sides, firm
square piers close the corners. The entrance is to the side next to the campa-
nile, and recalls in ornamentation Florentine quattrocento details. The apart-
ment house is lower and more in scale
with the surrounding streetscape. The
interior of the church proper is largely
undecorated, in keeping with the main
preaching function of the Baptist Church.
A series of brilliant stained-glass win-

*194. Stained-glass window by John La Farge*

dows by John La Farge help to continue
the coloration and excitement of the
exterior.

Somewhat the worse for wear, the Judson Church still serves the Greenwich
Village community.

195. *View from southwest, ca. 1904. In the distance are Mt. Prospect Reservoir water tower, the Brooklyn Museum and the reservoir headquarters building.*

## Grand Army Plaza and Soldiers' and Sailors' Memorial Arch
## Main Entrance to Prospect Park, Brooklyn, New York
## 1889–1901

The ensemble of arch and appendant structures at Grand Army Plaza in Brooklyn is one of the greatest and most successful patriotic, ritualistic centers ever created in America. It demonstrates the ideals of "civic art" and artistic collaboration, twin animating forces in much of McKim, Mead & White's urban architecture.

An oval-shaped plaza with suitable monuments was envisioned in the original plans Clavert Vaux and Frederick Law Olmsted drew up for Prospect Park in 1865–66. They saw the plaza as a transition zone between the "rural" atmosphere of the park and the city. Ten major roads converged near the park's entrance which made it necessary to create some sort of traffic separation. Intentions were for the plaza to be a public meeting place with a speaker's platform and a site for public rituals; however, the scale of the plaza, approximately 1,350 feet long and 900 feet wide, proved to be overwhelming. Beginning in the late 1860s and continuing throughout the 1870s various attempts to control the space were made, such as a fountain and a nine-foot-tall statue of Abraham Lincoln on a fifteen-foot base. By the mid-1880s the plaza was considered "a great failure . . . a stony waste . . . suggestive of Siberia in winter and

196. *Soldiers' and Sailors' Memorial Arch, ca. 1901*

197. *Plan*

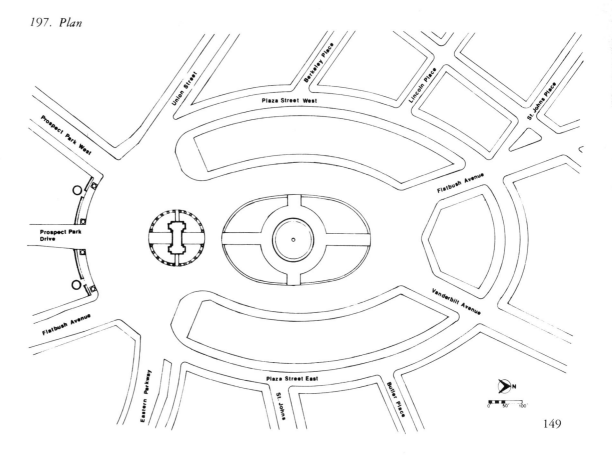

149

198. Navy *pedestal group*
*by Frederick MacMonnies*

Sahara in summer."[1] In 1885 the mayor of Brooklyn, Seth Low, had proposed an arch in honor of Civil War veterans be located in the plaza. After several years of political squabbles, a competition was held in 1889 and won by John H. Duncan. The arch without sculptures was completed in 1892. Modeled after the Arch of Titus in Rome, Duncan's arch stood 287 feet from the park's entrance. Eighty feet in height and width, the structure encloses an arch fifty feet high and spanning thirty-five feet.

Stanford White entered the scene in 1894. Since the late 1880s the firm had designed entrances and structures for Prospect Park (i.e., Willink Entrance, 1888–92; Lullwood Bridge, 1888–90; the base to the James S. T. Stranaham Monument, 1891—sculpture by Frederick MacMonnies—and many more). In concert with the park administrator, Frank Squier, White redesigned the plaza entrance making it into a national Valhalla for the Civil War. Concurrently, trolley tracks that used to run in front of the arch were relocated, and Olmsted's firm redesigned the plaza's planting and formalized the fountain's setting. White redesigned the arch so it could carry sculptures, and secured for his friend Frederick MacMonnies the commission for the triumphal *quadriga* (1898) on the top, and the twin groups of *Army* and *Navy* on the south pedestals. These bristling and vibrant sculptures were clearly influenced by Rude's work on the Arc de Triomphe in Paris. Below them on the pedestals between the columns are medallions representing several of the Army and Navy corps in

199. *Column at park entrance*

200. *O'Donovan and Eakin's* Lincoln

151

*201. Design for park entrance. Working drawing, ink on linen, signed "Ives, December 11, 1894."*

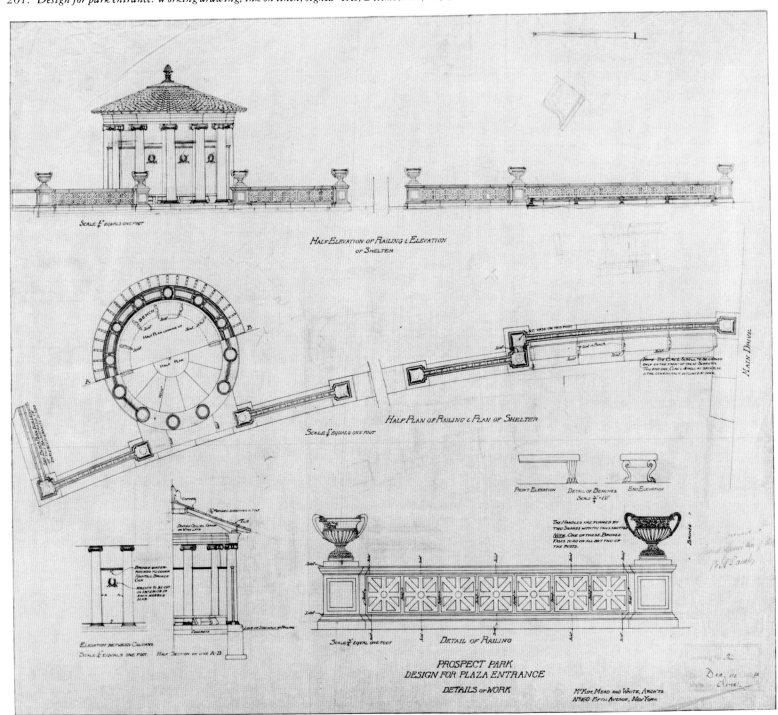

which Brooklyn men had served. The figures in the spandrel panels were provided by Philip Martiny. On either side beneath the arch, bas-reliefs of Lincoln and Grant mounted on horseback were products of a collaboration between Thomas Eakins for the horse and William O'Donovan for the figures. The arch was separated from the traffic by low granite bolsters connected by a bronze chain.

Eight bronze lamp standards marked entrances to the arch. The entire plaza was repaved in a Belgian block-granite pattern and a herringbone-brick pattern was laid at the park's entrance. The formal entrance into the park was widened, and four, fifty-foot-tall Doric columns on square bases, topped by bronze eagles (also by MacMonnies) were placed across the front. The bases of the columns were decorated by bundled *fascia* and eagles. Behind the columns a low pierced granite wall with bronze urns and benches was placed. At either corner twin Ionic-columned waiting stations with Guastavino-vaulted roofs provided shelter during inclement weather.

White's design greatly formalized the plaza and also improved the awkward proportions of the arch. Grand Army Plaza became the traditional celebratory center for patriotic holidays for many years. Recently, after years of neglect, the *quadriga* was restored; however, the apparent structures, urns, shelters and railings have suffered greatly from neglect.

[1] Brooklyn Park Commissioners, *Twenty Seventh Annual Report of the Department of Parks for the Year 1887* (Brooklyn, 1888), 28.

*202. Memorial Arch lamp standard*

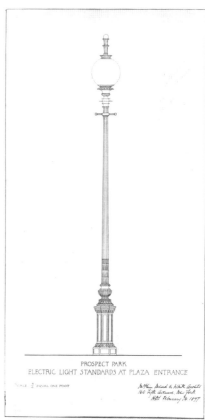

*203–204. Studies for electric light standards. Ink on linen.*

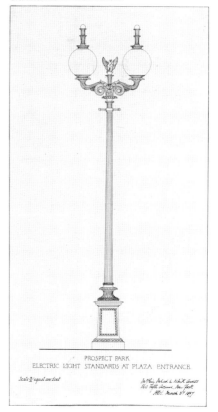

205. *West front approach*

## Hamilton McKown Twombly House and Farm Buildings
## "Florham"
285 Madison Avenue
Madison, New Jersey
1890–1900

Writing to Frank Millet, a artist/friend residing in England who McKim, Mead & White used as an antique procurer, William R. Mead observed: "Twombly wants a house on the order of an English Country gentleman. I don't think he knows exactly what he means, and I am sure I don't, but as near as I can gather, his idea is that it shall be a thoroughly comfortable house without the stiffness of the modern city house. Twombly is the sort of man, who, if he gets what he wants, is willing to pay liberally for it."[1]

Hamilton McKown Twombly was the husband of Florence Vanderbilt (the daughter of William H. Vanderbilt) and the business manager of the entire Vanderbilt family business interests between the late 1880s and his death in 1910. At Madison, New Jersey, he created a suitable country house ensemble as befitted his position at a total cost in excess of $700,000. In contrast to some of the other Vanderbilt brothers and sisters who actively sought publicity through their palace-building mania (i.e., Marble House, Biltmore, etc.), the Twomblys were extremely private and no photographs or plans of the house ever appeared in architectural journals or books. Comparatively unknown, the estate is one of the most elaborate ever constructed in the United States.[2]

206. *Garden, east rear*

207. *Door molding detail*

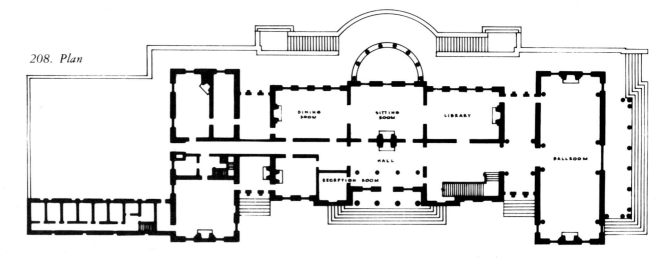

208. *Plan*

209. *Main hall, fireplace and mantel*

Beginning in 1890 Twombly began purchasing land in Madison, New Jersey. Located about twenty-five miles from Manhattan, the area provided easy access and yet retained a semi-rural character. In time he assembled a plot of about twelve hundred acres, which was bisected by a railroad. Twombly vacillated as to whether to renovate an older house located alongside the main highway, or jump the railroad tracks and build a large mansion within the grounds. All three McKim, Mead & White partners participated at various times in the designing of the estate, yet the decision of locating the house seems to have been primarily the work of Stanford White.[3] In support of his recommendation to locate the house within the property, White called up Frederick Law Olmsted. Olmsted wrote Twombly:

*The relation of a house to a property and land is one thing. The relation of a house to a property in landscape quite another. You are not the sort of man who would wish to make an ostentatious show of property* simply as property. *You want property in land about your house sufficient to secure spaciousness of effect and a sense of domestic freedom. You want to have it apparent to all that your domestic life is not liable to come under the scrutiny of what may be disagreeable gossiping neighbors, or be within earshot, either of such neighbors, or of idlers and strollers on a public road. You want*

210. *Main hall, ca. 1900. Visible are the copies of Roman emperors' busts and the Barberini tapestries.*

*. . . land enough . . . to make you profit against possible encroachments that would interfere with a full enjoyment of your property in landscape. . . . A big eminent and costly house should have more spacious landscape advantages than a small, secluded and demure cottage . . . you have a sweep of landscape to an infinitely remote and perspectively obscure background, an appropriate and well-proportioned foreground and middle distance being perfectly within your control; as much so as if you owned the State of New Jersey. . . . You have everything screened that is desirable to be screened. Everything within twenty miles is as much under your control, so far as concerns the fitness, propriety and becomingness of the situation, as if you had the free use of it. The grand landscape is yours and nobody can interfere with your possession of it.*[4]

The result was a large mansion with stables, orangerie and greenhouses and garden structures, a gatehouse, a model dairy farm, stud farm, and other elements of what was considered to be a country gentleman's estate. A special railroad siding was constructed for private railroad cars and also coal delivery. Three hundred acres were devoted to the house, garden and park, and the remaining nine hundred to farming. The farm became well known for its prize Guernsey cows.

Architecturally, the style chosen was English, a cross between Wren's work at Hampton Court and later eighteenth-century models. Mead was responsible for much of the design and for handling Twombly as a client. McKim designed the stable for the main house and probably the exterior of the house; White

211. *Garden pavilion to east*

212. Orangerie

certainly helped on the interior. The main hall was furnished with copies of busts of Roman emperors—Mead wrote to Millet: "I don't think Twombly cares so much for antiques but rather prefers new things made after known models."[5] One exception was a set of tapestries, the Barberini tapestries, made for King Louis XIII of France and presented to the papal legate Francesco Barberini. White procured the tapestries through a New York antique importer from the Uffizi Galleries in Florence.[6] Other interior furnishings consisted of portraits of English earls and dukes and authentic and imitation Chippendale furniture.

Twombly's evident intentions were to create an appropriate backdrop for an American noble family. Fate was not so kind, however; one daughter died young of typhoid fever, and the son, Hamilton Jr., died in a summer-camp accident in 1906. His father never recovered from the blow, resigned all his social and business interests and died in 1910.

Somewhat altered, the house and many of the outbuildings presently serve as the Madison campus for Fairleigh Dickinson College.

[1] Letter, Mead to Frank Millet, July 9, 1895, The New-York Historical Society.

[2] One exception is: Ellis R. Meeker, compiler, *New Jersey: A Historical, Commercial and Industrial Review* (Elizabeth, N.J.: Commonwealth, Pubs., 1906).

[3] Letters, Twombly to White, March 17, and May 12, 1890; letters John C. Olmsted to White, July 10, 18 and 31, and September 18, 1890, The New-York Historical Society.

[4] Letter, Frederick Law Olmsted to Twombly, April 3, 1891, The New-York Historical Society.

[5] Letter, Mead to Millet, July 9, 1895, The New-York Historical Society.

[6] Letter of Agreement between Stanford White and Charles M. Foulke, December 13, 1892, The New-York Historical Society.

213. *Rendering of farm complex by office of McKim, Mead & White*
214. *Gate house*

215. *View from northeast*

216. *Plan*

WALKER ART GALLERY, BOWDOIN COLLEGE, BRUNSWICK, MAINE

**Walker Art Building**
**Bowdoin College**
**Brunswick, Maine**
**1891–95**

Designed by Charles McKim, the Walker Art Building was intended to serve as the art gallery for the Bowdoin College campus. A tightly controlled rectangular structure, the interior divisions are clearly revealed in the front elevation. The deep insertion of the loggia and white limestone surrounds contrasts with the brick wings. The building recalls various Renaissance structures, such as the Pazzi Chapel, though the scale and placement on a terrace with a backdrop of trees, and a green lawn give the appearance of a garden casino. The motif of the central loggia has a possible source in the garden loggia of

the Villa Medici or the upper level of the Nymphaeum of the Villa Giulia, both in Rome. But as with all such features, changes of scale and also details have occurred. Befitting the high cultural aspirations of the art building, reproductions of *Demosthenes* at the Vatican and *Aeschines* at Naples are in the niches, and the porch rondels carry busts of *Olympia* and *Plato*.

The evocation of past cultures continued with the interior decoration. Daniel Chester French provided a Renaissance-inspired bronze relief of Theophilus Wheeler Walker, in whose memory the building was erected. Murals by four prominent American painters commemorating great artistic cultures of the past were placed in the four lunettes: *Venice* by Kenyon Cox, *Rome* by Elihu Vedder, *Florence* by Abbott Thayer and *Athens* by John La Farge.

217. *Rotunda with murals.*
*From left to right:*
Rome *by Elihu Vedder,*
Venice *by Kenyon Cox and*
Athens *by John La Farge.*

## Rhode Island State House
## 90 Smith Street
## Providence, Rhode Island
## 1891–1904

The construction of new state capitol buildings preoccupied Americans in the turn-of-the-century period and the Rhode Island State House became a prime model. While agitation for a new statehouse began in the 1850s, it was not until January 1890 that the state legislature appointed a New State House Commission.[1] The important members of the commission were the chairman, Governor and later ex-Governor, Herbert W. Ladd and Rowland G. Hazard III of Peacedale, Rhode Island. The commission visited New York in September 1890 to inspect various buildings and meet with several public officials and architects. They tried unsuccessfully to meet with McKim, Mead & White. Subsequently, McKim, Mead and several New York architects visited Providence to inspect various proposed statehouse sites. The commission also visited McKim's Boston Public Library, then under construction, and described in its first annual report a library that was a "magnificent structure of marble and granite, a model of architectural beauty and simplicity." A program for the new capitol building was written and a two-tier competition was determined in which the first round would be open only to Rhode Island firms, with the three best being asked to compete in a second round against selected firms from outside the state. The outcome of the competition was foregone. In a letter marked "confidential," Governor Ladd explained the politics of his situation to Charles McKim, and asked for advice.[2] The finalists were to receive one-thousand-dollar awards. The first round was announced in November 1890, with entries due in February 1891. The second round was announced in August 1891, and had entries due by January 14, 1892.

McKim, Mead & White were formally selected as the winners on February 10, 1892, and, after a campaign and vote on bonds for construction, selection of a site and some redesign, construction began in 1895. The cornerstone was laid on October 15, 1896. The orator for the ceremony was Rowland G. Hazard III. By December 1900, the building was sufficiently completed that offices began to occupy it, and the buildings and grounds were turned over to the state in June 1904. The builders were Norcross Brothers, of Worcester, Massachusetts; the original projected cost of $1 million rose to a final figure of some $3 million. Despite agitation by the press, no questionable financial dealings were ever proved, and, in fact, the building became known as an example of financial honesty in public buildings.[3]

The site of the new capitol, Smith's Hill, was not formally approved until 1894; all of the competitions were for an unnamed site with the same topographic characteristics as Smith's Hill. Clearly the favored site from the beginning, Smith's Hill was a tract of eighteen acres located adjacent to downtown, but never developed because of intervening

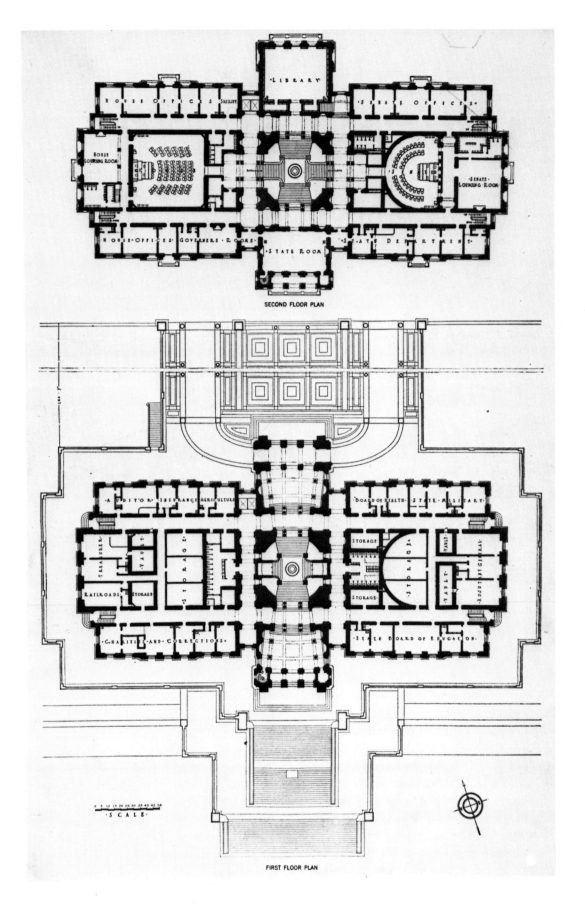

SECOND FLOOR PLAN

FIRST FLOOR PLAN

railroad tracks. After McKim, Mead & White won the competition, the Public Parks Association of Providence—a civic art group typical of the American Renaissance period—issued a booklet as part of the campaign for the new State House Bond Issue. In the booklet, they advocated the site of Smith's Hill as "commanding, quiet, convenient to the new passenger station, and to the business center of Providence, and hav[ing] ample grounds in front." The Public Parks Association went on: "We would suggest that an area three hundred feet wide from the passenger station to the Capitol be converted into a magnificent boulevard. What an ornament this would be to the city, to the State! How much it would add to the attractions of the State House! It would be one of the grandest boulevards in the country."[4] This conclusion, according to the booklet, was arrived at after studying numerous state capitols and their locations. McKim, Mead & White participated in the campaign on the bond issue and commissioned Hughson Hawley, a noted architectural renderer, to provide a colored drawing.[5]

The competition was judged by the State House Commission. Assisting them on deciding how well the entries met the program and influencing the artistic selection as well, were Richard Morris Hunt, a New York architect; Professor A.D.F. Hamlin of the Columbia College School of Architecture; and A. C. Morse, dean of Providence architects. Hamlin had previously worked in the McKim, Mead & White office. Hunt was an old friend of the firm and was

*220. Longitudinal section. Ink on linen, signed, "H. Bacon, March 20, 1895."*

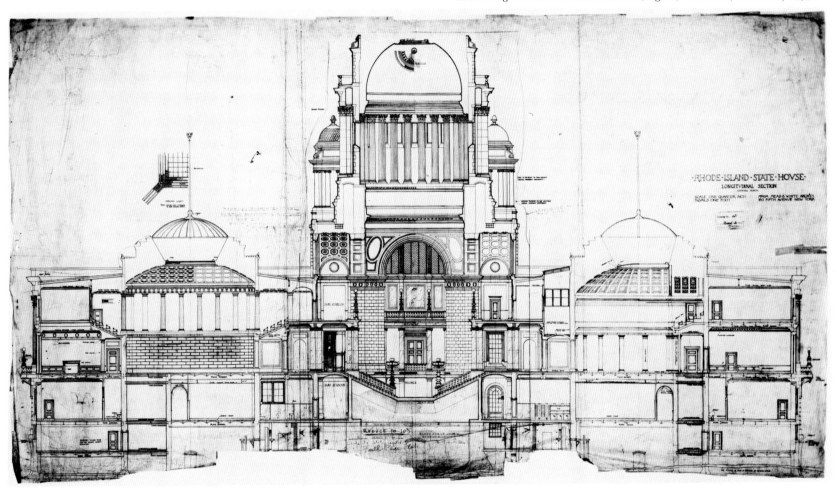

working closely with McKim at that time on the World's Columbian Exposition in Chicago. Hunt's role in selecting the winner is confirmed in a letter by Rowland G. Hazard (who had just commissioned McKim to design his house): *The chief consulting architect, Mr. Richard Hunt of New York, was most highly entertaining in the way in which he handled the plans put into the competition. He has a way of whistling in his conversation which*

*is very significant and impossible to write. He is also a remarkably fine looking man and can make more faces in the furtherance of his ideas than anybody I happen to have seen lately. It was better than a play to look at him and to see the petrified countenances of some of the country members of the commission. We all voted without any dissent in favor of McKim, and I confess to being greatly impressed with the stately classical lines of his plans. Besides having beauty of*

165

221. *Rotunda*

*exterior, it is most skillfully managed as to its interior arrangements. In particular, the feature of the building being the main hall, which is splendidly lighted and would make a place fit for the names of our most celebrated men.*[6]

The other entries either harkened back to the picturesque medievalism and massing of the 1870s and 1880s, or attempted to use classicism, but in a clumsy, unknowledgeable way.[7] Plans in general were inept. The McKim, Mead & White winning entry presented a monumentally classical building with a solidity, appropriate centrality and articulation, though not extreme, of the different internal spaces. The commission cited the "artistic effect and practical arrangement. . . . The building is monumental in character and of a classic type, as most closely associated with the best civic examples." Clearly the favorite entry, the design was reviewed by the Providence *Journal* in late January 1892, along with all the others, and described as "a splendid example of composition, according to the purest ideas of Renaissance." The plan in particular was admired for its compact organization with the rotunda serving as the major vertical communication space, and the arrangement of the two legislative houses and governor's suite on the upper floor. In a letter to Professor Eugene Letang of M.I.T., McKim responded to praise: "I have had some hand in the composition . . . to Mr. Mead belongs the credit of the arrangement of the plan which you like so much."[8]

In 1895, before beginning construction, some design modifications were

222. *Dome*

made. Two bays were added to each of
the wings, so increasing the length that
the central three bays of the wings were
enframed with pilasters that repeated
the motif of the entrance pavilions. The
depth of both entrance pavilions was
increased and into the north pavilion the
state library was placed on the upper
floor. Replacing the monitor domes for
the legislative chambers on the original
design were low-rising, Roman saucer
domes. Finally, on the exterior much of
the ornament was simplified and some
sculpture eliminated. On the interior,
most of the new space went into addi-
tional offices. A major change in the
circulation system occurred in the rotunda, where curving staircases were
eliminated; instead the visitor came up
short staircases from the vestibules to a
landing in the rotunda, then changed
direction to rise on axis to the legislative
chambers. The drama and centrality of
the rotunda was increased. Initially projected to be built of either Indiana limestone or Rhode Island granite, the final
material was white Georgia marble,
which Hunt convinced the commission
to substitute. Finally, in 1898, the
diameter of the dome was increased by
five feet in an attempt to match the size
of the Minnesota State Capitol then under construction.[9]

In form and general style, McKim
reached back to the American tradition
of the domed public building for the
statehouse. While a relationship is evident to the United States Capitol and
other statehouses, McKim typically was
both more scholarly and transformed
his details. A former office draughtsman

later claimed that McKim took some exterior details from "the little City Hall in New York City." McKim had admired the building and published a photograph in 1876 with the explanation: "It is a very fair specimen of the Renaissance of the time, and, on the whole, is the most admirable public building in the city."[10] Before the alterations of 1895 took place, the treatment of the wall and fenestration in the hyphens in New York and the wings in Providence were similar. The Providence dome was based on St. Paul's in London, though much smaller. Another possible source, St. Isaac's in St. Petersburg, was pointed out in 1898 by a Providence architect. St. Isaac's had originally been designed in 1817 by the French architect Auguste Ricard Monferrand.[11] The statue *Hope,* later retitled *Independent Man,* on top of the lantern was created by George T. Brewster. It was cast in bronze by the Gorham Manufacturing Company.

McKim intended an elaborate interior decoration, with collaboration among various artists, somewhat along the lines of the Boston Public Library; however, only a small amount of this was actually carried out. The renderings for the different lamps are some indication of the quality McKim sought. Elmer Garnsey did the decorative painting throughout, and in the 1940s Giorgio de Felice added the Raphaelesque embellishments to the rotunda.[12] Only the governor's reception room continues the richness of the rotunda with its Louis Quatorze style. The rotunda is clearly the major space of the interior, with the white marble stairs, balconies, balustrades and bronze *torcheres.* The contrast in scale between the huge piers and the columns supporting the balconies emphasizes the monumental aspirations, and the monocolor, relieved by touches of color from the bronze and the decorative painting, gives it a ceremonial character recalling great architectural feats of the past.

The projected grand boulevard, or parade ground, that was to make the connection with downtown was never carried out; consequently, the statehouse remains isolated from downtown by the railroad tracks, a "temple in the railyard." Gleaming white and restrained, the completed building dominates Providence—the focus is appropriately on the dome, surrounded by the four domed *tourelles,* with the deep ceremonial loggia below for official pronouncements. It illuminates the aesthetic and historical goals of the American Renaissance, recalling Rome of both the emperors and the Renaissance, the London of Wren and the American classical heritage, while many of the carved details have a French delicacy and feeling. Appropriate inscriptions in the attic of each portico outline the history of the state and make connections to principles of government. Both the exterior inscriptions are in English. On the interior in the entablature of the dome a Latin inscription appears.[13] This selection of many aspects of the past, recombined in a new whole, is typical of McKim, Mead & White's scientific eclecticism.

The statehouse still exists in fairly good condition.

*224. Plan for grounds and approaches*

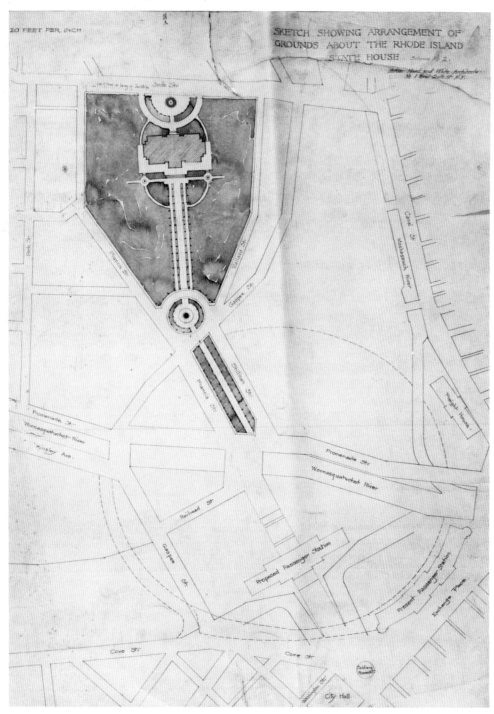

[1]  Primary research materials are in The New-York Historical Society and the Rhode Island State Archives. See also, Henry-Russell Hitchcock and William Seale, *Temples of Democracy, The State Capitols of the U.S.A.* (New York: Harcourt Brace Jovanovich, 1976), ch. 6; and my entry in William Jordy and Christopher Monkhouse, *Buildings on Paper* (Providence, R.I.: Brown University, the Rhode Island Historical Society and the Rhode Island School of Design, 1982), 115–17.

[2]  Letter, Ladd to McKim, November 26, 1890, The New-York Historical Society.

[3]  "A Monument to Honesty," *Cincinnati Post*, July 6, 1904, typescript copy in The New-York Historical Society.

[4]  Public Parks Association of Providence, *Rhode Island State House on Smith's Hill. Grand Boulevard No. 10* (1892): 3, 5.

[5]  "Hughson Hawley, Scenic Artist and Architectural Painter," *Pencil Points* 9 (December 1928): 761–74.

[6]  Catherine Hazard, ed., *Letters of Rowland Gibson Hazard* (Boston: D. B. Updike, 1922).

225. *"Temple in the Railyards." View from the center of Providence.*

7   Illustrations of the competition projects by: McKim, Mead & White; Sheply, Rutan & Coolidge of Boston; Carrère & Hastings and J. C. Cady of New York; William R. Walker & Son, Stone, Carpenter & Wilson, and Hoppin, Read & Hoppin of Providence; and Gould & Angle of Newport, can be found in the Providence *Journal,* January 28, 1892; and *The American Architect and Building News* 35 (February 13, 1892), no. 842.

8   Letter, McKim to Letang, February 29, 1892, The New-York Historical Society.

9   Letter, Glazer to Norcross Brothers, June 13, 1898, The New-York Historical Society. The State House Commission was very proud that the dome was of masonry construction and today it is, with the Taj Mahal, St. Peter's and the Minnesota State Capitol, one of the four largest structurally integral marble domes in the world.

10   Hitchcock and Seale, *Temples,* 218; and *The New York Sketch Book of Architecture* 3 (July 1876), op. pl. 25. In the basement of the State House there are remains of a model that illustrates an intermediate project.

11   Letter, Hoffman to McKim, Mead & White, October 24, 1898, The New-York Historical Society.

12   Contracts with Garnsey signed, November 21, 1899, October 26, 1900, The New-York Historical Society. The four pendentive and the dome murals are signed by George de. Felice and dated, AD MCMXLVII.

13   The inscription in the south attic reads: "To hold forth a lively experiment that a most flourishing civil state may stand and best be maintained with full liberty in religious concernments" (from the Royal Charter of 1663). In the north attic appears: "Providence Plantation Founded by Roger Williams, 1636; Providence-Portsmouth-Newport Incorporated by Parliament, 1643; Rhode Island-Providence Plantations Obtained Royal Charter, 1663; In General Assembly Declared a Sovereign State, May 4, 1776." The interior inscription reads: "Rara temporum felicitas ubi sentire quae velis et quae sentias dicere licet" (Rare felicity to the times when it is permitted to think as you like and to say what you think).

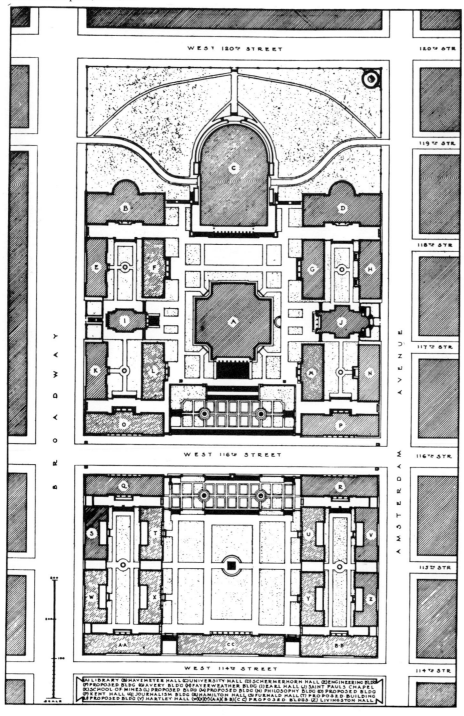

226. *Block plan, ca. 1915*

WEST 120TH STREET

120TH STR

119TH STR

118TH STR

117TH STR

116TH STR

115TH STR

114TH STR

WEST 116TH STREET

WEST 114TH STREET

BROADWAY

AMSTERDAM AVENUE

(A) LIBRARY (B) HAVEMEYER HALL (C) UNIVERSITY HALL (D) SCHERMERHORN HALL (E) ENGINEERING BLDG
(F) PROPOSED BLDG (G) AVERY BLDG (H) FAYERWEATHER BLDG (I) EARL HALL (J) SAINT PAULS CHAPEL
(K) SCHOOL OF MINES (L) PROPOSED BLDG (M) PROPOSED BLDG (N) PHILOSOPHY BLDG (O) PROPOSED BLDG
(P) KENT HALL (Q) JOURNALISM BLDG (R) HAMILTON HALL (S) FURNALD HALL (T) PROPOSED BUILDING
(U) PROPOSED BLDG (V) HARTLEY HALL (W)(X)(Y)(AA)(BB)(CC) PROPOSED BLDGS (Z) LIVINGSTON HALL

SCALE

172

**Columbia University**
**Morningside Heights**
**Broadway at 116th Street**
**New York, New York**
**1892–1901 First Stage**
**1903–1930 Second Stage**

In 1892 Columbia College (renamed Columbia University in 1896) decided to move the campus from Fifth Avenue and Forty-ninth Street to the Upper West Side on Morningside Heights. The site, still largely suburban and the highest point on Manhattan Island, took up four blocks between Amsterdam Avenue and Broadway and between 116th and 120th Streets. The Board of Trustees and the college president, Seth Low (a former mayor of Brooklyn and later mayor of New York) engaged Richard Morris Hunt, Charles Coolidge Haight and McKim, Mead & White (with McKim as the representative) to jointly draw up a plan. Collaboration proved impossible and each submitted individual proposals in April 1893. These greatly diverged. Haight and Hunt differed markedly in stylistic terms—Haight proposed the English Gothic while Hunt advocated the Italian Renaissance—yet both saw the campus as an enclosed series of courts with an inward focus. McKim argued for a scheme located on a high podium with a large central building that would be oriented towards the south and towards the central city. The trustees favored certain aspects of each scheme, though McKim's seems to have been the favorite, and they asked Wil-

227. *Low Library. In front, on the stairs, is Daniel Chester French's* Alma Mater. *At left are the School of Mines and Earl Hall.*

liam Robert Ware, the head of the School of Architecture, Alexander Trowbridge, an architecture professor, and Frederick Law Olmsted to combine the best aspects of each: "The large accommodation and open external courts of Mr. Hunt's scheme, and the practical convenience and ample provision for lecture rooms shown in Mr. Haight's, with the symmetry and monumental disposition of Mr. McKim's."[1] McKim and Ware did not particularly get along in architectural matters, and McKim went to work behind the scenes to influence others.[2] After a period of infighting, McKim threatened to resign, and in December 1893 his firm was selected as architects for the entire development.[3]

The style of the new campus buildings had been a point of controversy and each of the architects had recommended a different approach. The trustees went to some lengths to analyze the best response and finally decided the classic "will appeal most strongly to educated popular taste, and will be most likely to secure an imposing architectural effect." Any attempt to use the Gothic, the trustees wrote, would seem "to be imitating the English universities, and shall thereby suggest a comparison which can scarcely fail to be unfavorable to us."[4] In choosing McKim, the trustees firmly rejected any compromise with the Gothic.

McKim envisioned the heights as a great podium, a virtual acropolis of New

173

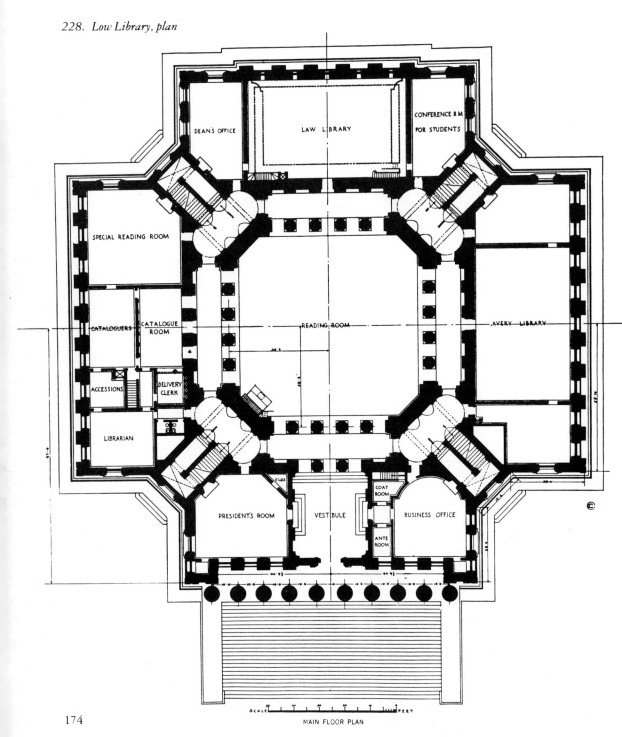

228. *Low Library, plan*

Within the plan, the following labels appear:

DEAN'S OFFICE · LAW LIBRARY · CONFERENCE R M FOR STUDENTS · SPECIAL READING ROOM · CATALOGUERS · CATALOGUE ROOM · READING ROOM · AVERY LIBRARY · ACCESSIONS · DELIVERY CLERK · LIBRARIAN · PRESIDENT'S ROOM · VESTIBULE · COAT ROOM · ANTE ROOM · BUSINESS OFFICE · CLOS

SCALE · FEET

MAIN FLOOR PLAN

York City. The major building, the library, would be the central element, and the entrance to the campus would be on 116th Street and not on one of the long avenues. Further changes in the plan occurred in mid-1894 when President Seth Low made it known that he would make a gift of $1 million to the library in memory of his father. Redesigns for the library occurred throughout the remainder of 1894, creating the present domed Low Library. Buildings around it assumed more of a deferential character. Construction of the campus north of 116th Street began in 1895, and by 1898 the Low Library, Havemeyer, Fayerweather, Schermerhorn and the engineering halls were largely complete. Small additions continued past the turn of the century, and then in 1903, the university having acquired the land south of 116th Street, hired McKim, Mead & White to make additions to the campus. This 1903 "Block Plan" was subsequently published with the date 1893.[5] The plan significantly altered the campus—enclosed, albeit at a lower level, the original panoramic expanse to the south. During this time, 116th Street was closed to vehicular traffic, and enclosure and separation from the city was further emphasized. The firm continued to add buildings following McKim's original scheme and style: the Avery Library (1911–12), Kent Hall (1909–11) and others. In 1934, the Low Library became primarily an administrative and research center and a new library, the Butler, by James Gambrel Rogers, was constructed at the south end of the new campus addition. In the 1950s and later,

MEDICINE

229. Low Library

230. *Havemeyer Hall*

architects and campus planners worked at the fringes of McKim's scheme, though the central integrity was preserved.

McKim's vision for the campus seems to have evolved over a period of time. The concept of a raised central domical building, of course, has a long history in Western architecture and in American campus design—it appears in Jacque Louis Ramee's Union College and Thomas Jefferson's University of Virginia. (McKim, Mead & White worked on the University of Virginia beginning in late 1895.) McKim's design, while certainly indebted to all of these sources and many more, remained essentially his own creation, a response to a specific site and requirement. He saw the campus as one large space, different areas defined by different boundaries, some covered, others open. He did not differentiate spaces as quadrangles in the English manner, but rather saw the campus as a series of related spaces, defined by buildings, and more abstract elements: terraces, steps, planters, balustrades, benches, pavement patterns, grass and fountains.

The buildings, with the exception of the Low Library, are simply backdrops to the processional nature of movement; it is a campus to be experienced through walking. The Low Library and the statue in front, Daniel Chester French's *Alma Mater* (1900–03, its base by McKim) are the focal points. From all points one is ultimately pulled toward the Low with its great Ionic portico and granite columns sitting on white marble bases, and the statue with its uplifted arms. Movement is not necessarily on axis, and in-

deed one reaches the campus on the cross axis of 116th Street. The consequence is diagonal movement through a series of spaces. Frequently, unacknowledged but of essential support to the campus are the "utilitarian" classroom and faculty office buildings such as Havemeyer and Schermerhorn halls. Stylistically they are vaguely French in their feeling with their red brick and limestone details. Tall and somewhat thin, they provide the suitable background vertical accents for the campus.

The Low Library served a double function, both as a library and as the ritualistic center of the campus, the holy center of learning. Significantly when a chapel was added it was off to the side, and designed by Howells & Stokes (1903–07) one of the few early buildings not by McKim, Mead & White. Frequently compared to a variety of sources such as the Pantheon, the Library of Congress and the Rotunda at University of Virginia, the final design of the library was peculiarly McKim's solution. As a functional library it never worked very well, controlled by the powerful abstract geometry. The plan is essentially a Greek cross, the void at the center used for the reading room is the dominant element. This is surrounded by an ambulatory, and the other functions of the library, such as specialized reading rooms, catalogue and stacks, are pushed into the wings. The consequence is a procession to the center; the dome and space overpower while directional orientation to the necessities, such as looking up a book, are afterthoughts. On the exterior, the building has certain features typical of McKim. While details

such as the moldings or the antifixae on the cornice of the drum are particularly refined, there is a certain primitivism to McKim's composition. He has combined together a number of primary compositional elements: the too-heavy portico and tall attic, the high walls of the other three arms, the drum opened by the large thermal windows, and then on top a low Roman saucer dome. Only the details are refined, the rest of the building has a powerful, rude strength of classicism being reborn.

McKim's Columbia campus and the Low Library have to rank as one of the finest American designs, a totality where each part works towards a whole. In the pavement in front of the Low Library near *Alma Mater*, a memorial to McKim is placed in the pavement. The Latin inscription reads:

DESVPER ARTIFICIS
SPECTANT MONUMENTA
PER ANNOS[6]

[1] Trustees of Columbia University, *Report on the New Site and Buildings 1891–1898* (New York: Columbia University Press, 1898). The entire sequence of the design development until 1898 is conveniently summarized in Francesco Passanti, "The Design of Columbia in the 1890s, McKim and His Client," *Journal of the Society of Architectural Historians* XXXVI (May 1977): 69–84; however, my conclusions differ significantly from Mr. Passanti's. See also, John William Robson, *A Guide to Columbia University With Some Account of its History and Traditions* (New York: Columbia University Press, 1937).

[2] Letters reprinted in Charles Moore, *The Life and Times of Charles Follen McKim* (Boston and New York: Houghton Mifflin Co., 1929), 264–65.

[3] Frederick P. Hill, *Charles F. McKim: the Man* (Francestown, N.H.: privately printed, 1950), 18–19.

[4] *Report on New Site*, n.p.

[5] *A Monograph on the Works of McKim, Mead & White, 1879–1915* (New York: Architectural Book Publishing Company, 1915–1920), vol. 1, plate 47.

[6] "The Monuments look down upon us throughout the ages."

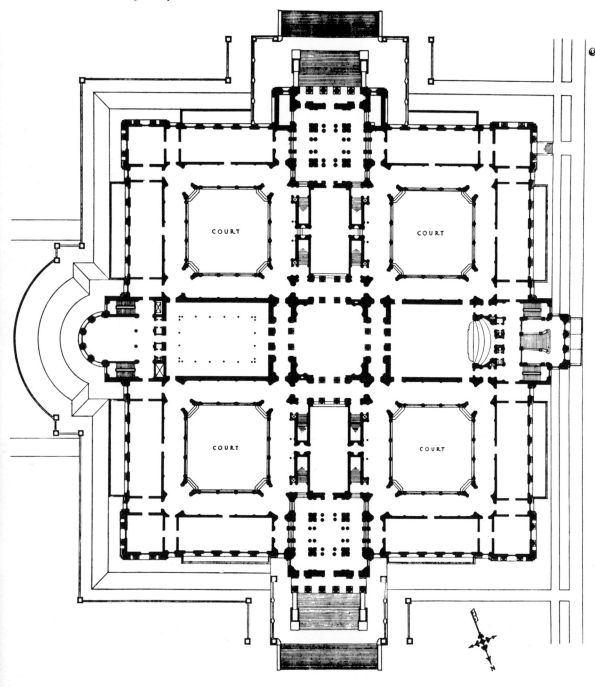

**Brooklyn Institute of Arts and Sciences**
**188 Eastern Parkway**
**Brooklyn, New York**
**1893–1927**

The Brooklyn Museum traces its history back to 1835 and the founding of the old Brooklyn Institute. By the late 1880s the mania for large civic cultural institutions seduced Brooklyn's cultural and political leaders, and agitation began for a museum to rival the recently founded Metropolitan Museum of Art and American Museum of Natural History across the river in Manhattan. The leader of the drive was Professor Franklin W. Hooper who became the museum's first director and curator. In 1890 the New York State Legislature passed incorporating legislation for the new Brooklyn Institute of Arts and Sciences. In 1892 a site was obtained along Eastern Parkway in the area Olmsted and Vaux had set aside for public buildings in their Prospect Park plans of 1865. The new institute set up several departments in 1890, one of which was a Department of Architecture. On its advisory board were McKim and Mead, along with several present or former office employees: William Boring, John Carrère, Thomas Hastings and A.D.F. Hamlin. Under the direction of Hamlin, a two-tier competition was dreamed up. The first round—a non-paying sketch problem—would be open to everybody. The second round was open to the two winners of the first round and four se-

232. *Plaster model, ca. 1895*

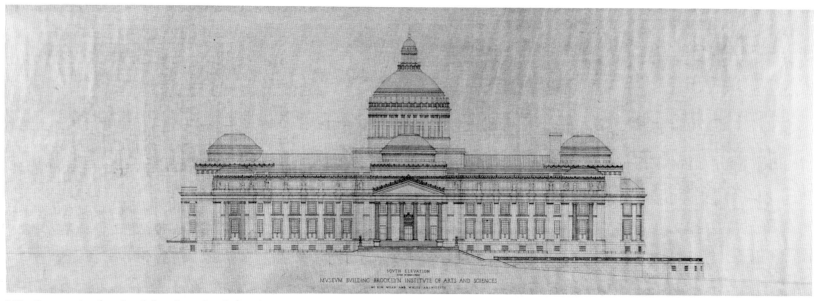

233. *Presentation drawing, ink on linen. South elevation.*

lected firms: McKim, Mead & White, J. C. Cady, Parfett Brothers and Carrère & Hastings. The final competition would be judged by Hamlin, Hooper, Robert W. Peabody of Boston (an old Ecole friend of McKim's) and George L. Morse, architect of Brooklyn. The first round became primarily a student exercise and was won by William Boring and Edward Tilton—members of the McKim office—and Brockway & Cromwell. McKim, Mead & White easily won the closed competition in May 1893, and construction began on the northwest wing in 1895.[1] This was opened in 1897. The Eastern Parkway front was completed in 1906 and construction of the McKim-designed building continued into the 1920s. By 1927 approximately one sixth of the projected scheme was completed. In the 1930s unsympathetic

additions and remodelings, including the removal of the monumental staircase, butchered McKim's original design.

McKim was the partner-in-charge of the museum's design. He envisioned possibly the world's largest museum, a building that would contain in its four main floors and basement over 500,000 square feet of space. The structure would have been 560 feet on a side. The central axis marked by the two main, north and south entrances would be a monumental sculptural hall, terminating in an 80-foot-in-diameter and 180-foot-high rotunda. The cross axis would contain an exhibition hall and an auditorium for twenty-five hundred people. The four corner courts would be each one hundred feet square and interior galleries would be forty feet wide.

Between the 1893 competition and the

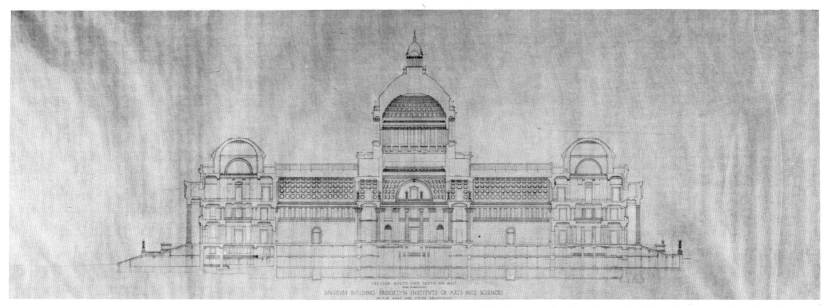

234. *Presentation drawing, ink on linen. Section, north and south on axis.*

beginning of construction in 1895, minor modifications were made to McKim's plan. The low Roman saucer dome was replaced by a high-profiled, Renaissance-styled dome surmounting a drum with a continuous colonnade. Also, in the redesign some of the exterior sculptural embellishments such as the twenty-foot-tall *quadrigas* on the corner pavilions were eliminated. The treatment of the elevations followed the scheme worked out by McKim for his almost-contemporaneous Agricultural Building at the Chicago World's Exposition. Central pavilions with subordinate low saucer domes would be articulated with temple porticos for the major entrances and curving excedras for the other two facades. The wings of seven bays and corner pavilions would have pilasters and engaged columns, and carry a tall attic. The main cornice breaking forward over each structural member would support sculptural figures twelve feet tall.

The decorating program was integral to the scheme. Each facade would portray certain historical periods and ideals, and indicate the interior program of that particular section of the museum. Thus the two facades of the northeast quadrant would contain Oriental Ideals, and the two facades of the northwest quadrant, Greek and Roman Ideals. Below in the frieze in large Roman letters would be carved names of great figures from the period. As constructed, the north entrance facade on Eastern Parkway contained one-half of the Greek and Roman and Oriental Ideals. The sculptor, Daniel Chester French, was put in charge of the decorative program and ultimately thirty

181

235. *Fourth-floor painting gallery, ca. 1907*

236. *Northeast court, ca. 1910, with* Bacchanti *by Frederick MacMonnies on display*

238. *Third-floor sculpture gallery, ca. 1904. The plaster model for the museum can be seen on display.*

monolithic statues representing *Greek Epic Poetry, Roman Law, Chinese Religion*, by a variety of sculptors, including Karl Bitter, Kenyon Cox, Janet Scudder and Edward C. Potter were installed.[2] The pediment by French was designed in concert with McKim and Hooper. It portrays two central figures, a man representing *Science* and a woman for *Art*, who holds a shield with the insignia of the institute. To the right three figures symbolize *Painting, Sculpture* and *Architecture*, and in the angle of the pediment a peacock stands, a symbol of Oriental art. Similarly, to the left three figures represent *Astronomy, Geology* and *Biology* and an Egyptian sphinx crouches in the angles, an Oriental symbol of wisdom.

Even though only a small portion of McKim's design was ever erected, and that has been castrated, enough remains to capture the ennobling vision of McKim, his partners and their patrons. Today the building still exists, though it is badly in need of restoration.

[1] "The Institute's Museum," *The Bulletin of the Brooklyn Institute of Arts & Sciences* II (February 20, 1909): 104–06 and (March 6, 1909): 159–60.

[2] "The Institute's Sculptures," *The Bulletin of the Brooklyn Institute of Arts & Sciences* I (October 10, 1908): 84; and McKim, Mead & White, *Brooklyn Institute Scrapbook*, Avery Architectural Library, Columbia University.

237. *Eastern Parkway (north) facade, ca. 1906*

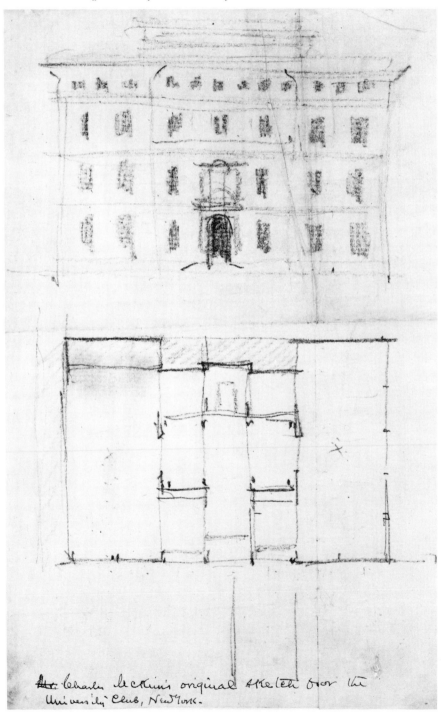

Charles McKim's original sketch for the University Club, New York.

## University Club
## 1 West Fifty-fourth Street
## New York, New York
## 1896–1900

McKim, Mead & White were the club architects for New York City in the turn-of-the-century period, designing or providing alterations for eight of the largest and most prestigious private men's clubs. The University Club by Charles McKim is one of the most prominent and most clearly reveals the creative qualities of the firm's eclecticism.[1] A preliminary sketch by McKim illustrated his approach to the design problems, or as his assistant Henry Bacon described: "In the sketch his idea was evident, but most indefinitely drawn, and in no stage of planning and designing did he make a definite line or contour."[2] McKim outlined the basic shape and bays of the building and onto this would be added features which were derived from various Italian Renaissance palazzi. No specific palazzo provided the overall source, rather the design was an eclectic assimilation of the cornice of the Palazzo Strozzi, the entrance of the Palazzo Borghese and numerous others. In the final design the apparent height was increased by allowing the intermediate floors, or mezzanines, and the attic floor to be expressed on the exterior, rather than be hidden as in most Italian examples. McKim also shrank the depth of the cornice allowing the building to gain in apparent height and to compete with its high-rise neighbors.

241. *Lounging room*

242. *Main hall*

Placed in panels between the intermediate floor windows were seals of American universities carved by Daniel Chester French and Kenyon Cox. Originally the club was separated from the street by a low balustrade. The building material was a pink Milford granite.

The plan was organized around an enclosed cortille that received different treatment on alternating floors, beginning as a full colonnade on the first floor, becoming a three-sided colonnade on the second floor and shrinking to four piers on the third floor. The main hall has polished green Connemarra marble columns and piers, with bases of Istrian stone and bronze capitals. Other stone used in the main hall for trim and the floor included white Norwegian marble, pink Knoxville marble and black Irish marble. Other interior spaces were equally impressive in their treatments. The great dining room is panelled in

*243. Floor plans*

McKIM, MEAD & WHITE

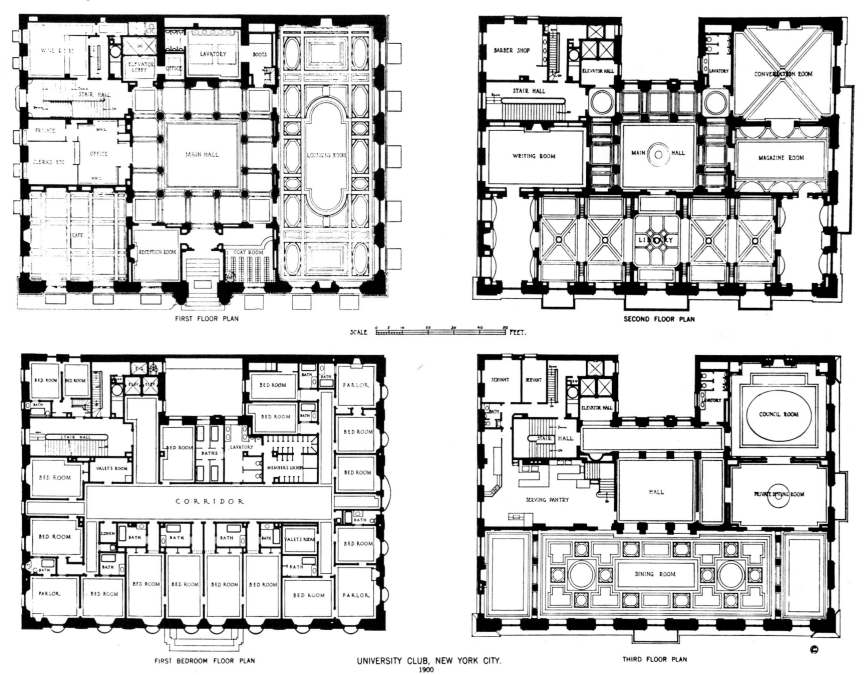

FIRST FLOOR PLAN

SECOND FLOOR PLAN

SCALE ⌊⊥⊥⊥⊥⊥⊥⊥⊥⊥⊥⊥⊥⊥⊥⊥⊥⊥⊥⊥⊥⊥⊥⊥⊥⊥⊥⊥⊥⌋ FEET.

FIRST BEDROOM FLOOR PLAN

UNIVERSITY CLUB, NEW YORK CITY.
1900

THIRD FLOOR PLAN

University Club

244. *Dining room*

245. *Library, showing the ceiling as was originally designed, ca. 1900*

wood. The centerpiece of the design, appropriate for a club of learning, is the library on the second floor, and here no expense was spared. In a long, barrel-vaulted room with cross-groin vaults, H. Siddons Mowbray provided a series of murals based on the decorations by Pinturicchio in the Borgia apartments in Rome. The rich deep color of the paintings and the tooled leather are evocative, and supposedly Le Corbusier on a visit in 1935 declared he could understand how one would become a Beaux-Arts architect, or as he wrote: "In New York, then, I learn to appreciate the Italian Renaissance. It is so well done that you could not believe it *to be genuine.* It even has a strange new firmness which is not Italian, but American!"[3]

[1] James W. Alexander, *A History of the University Club of New York* (New York: The University Club, 1915); and Charles Moore, *The Life and Times of Charles Follen McKim* (New York and Boston: Houghton Mifflin Co., 1929), ch. XIX.

[2] Henry Bacon, "Charles Follen McKim—A Character Sketch," *The Brickbuilder* 19 (February 1910): 38.

[3] Le Corbusier, *When Cathedrals Were White,* trans. F. E. Hyslop (New York: McGraw-Hill, 1964), 60.

246. *Library, ca. 1981*

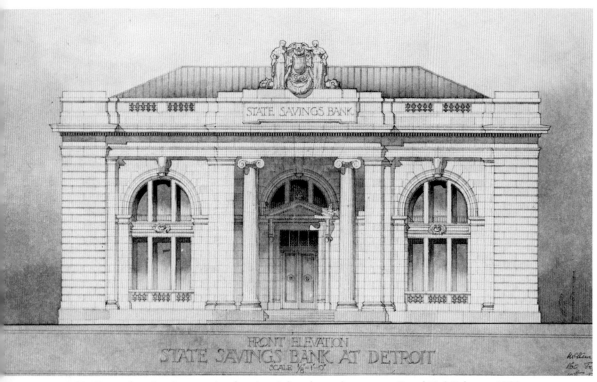

247. *Front elevation. Presentation drawing, ink and gouache on paper. Dated 19th February 1898.*

**State Savings Bank**
**Fort and Shelby Streets**
**Detroit, Michigan**
**1898–1900**

In 1898 Stanford White became involved in two projects in Detroit: the State Savings Bank and the Detroit Bicentennial Memorial. Behind both were a group of wealthy Detroit railway businessmen, art collectors and politicians: Charles Lang Freer, Frank J. Hecker, Senator James A. McMillan and George Russell. Freer, Hecker and McMillan were partners in the Peninsular Railroad Car Company (in 1899 the American Car and Foundry Company) and directors of the bank. Russell, also in railroad manufacturing business, acted as the bank's president. Lack of funds prevented construction of the Bicentennial Memorial. However, the bank was constructed and admirably served the objective of conveying a safe and conservative posture, providing links to the classical past and local boosterism.

White came to Detroit in 1898 at the request of Charles Freer. As a noted art collector, Freer had probably known White through mutual artist friends. A dinner to introduce White to the bank's officers was held at Freer's house and then "Mr. Freer had the table cleared and architect White proceeded to sketch a building on the beautiful banquet cloth."[1] All were so struck by White's enthusiasm that he was commissioned on the spot. Philip Sawyer was the firm's job captain and supervised construction.[2]

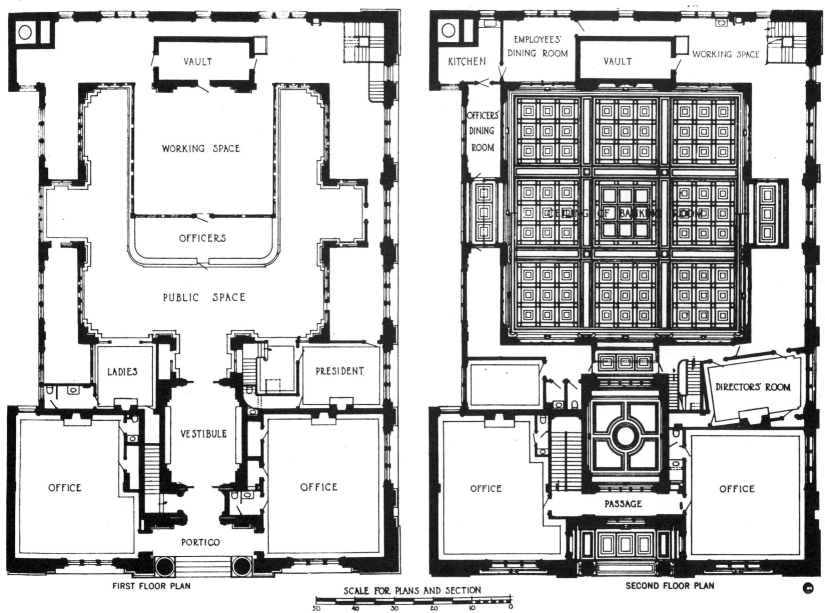

FIRST FLOOR PLAN

SECOND FLOOR PLAN

SCALE FOR PLANS AND SECTION

50　40　30　20　10　0

THE STATE SAVINGS BANK, DETROIT, MICHIGAN

1900

249. *Interior*

holding the seal of the state of Michigan.

The entrance sequence was a processional route of contrasting spaces, colors and materials: a twelve-foot-deep portico, a small entrance hall, a vestibule twenty-seven feet long covered by a mosaic-sheeted dome with an oculus, and then finally, the two-story banking room with tellers' wickets and counter screens which guarded the vault. Over the vault, as almost an altar painting, a lunette-shaped mural by Thomas Wilmer Dewing hovered. Dewing was a friend of White's and Freer eagerly collected Dewing's work and used the occasion to have him provide some decoration for his house.[3] The mural consisted of three colossal female figures in gowns; the central figure was *Detroit* who looks into the future, she was surrounded by *Commerce* and *Agriculture*. Coloration of the main banking room consisted of white Indiana marble, mosaic floors in black and red, highly polished bronze and a deep red and bright gold coffered ceiling. Images of security, profitability and conservative good sense provided an environment in which the bank's customers could act out their rituals. Alberti's prototype was never put to a more appropriate usage.

Recently the building was purchased by Silver's, an office-supply and gifts-store enterprise, and converted into a retail outlet and offices.

A local Detroit firm, Donaldson & Meier who had Beaux-Arts ties were local associates.

Rejecting the high-rise or skyscraper formula, White designed an exquisitely detailed strongbox. His model was Alberti's Tempio Malatestiano in Rimini. A series of strong arches contained the banking functions, giving way at the front for a deeply recessed portico. The superimposition of a second floor was clearly shown, and yet not allowed to dominate the composition. Construction was steel frame and brick with a white Indiana marble sheathing. The twin entrance Ionic columns were monolithic and weighed twenty-eight tons apiece. Over the entrance a sculpture by Philip Martiny portrays *Industry* and *Commerce*

[1] "A History of the State Savings Bank," in files of Manufacturers State Bank, Detroit.

[2] Philip Sawyer, *Edward Palmer York* (Stonington, Conn.: privately printed, 1951), 28–29.

[3] Letter, Charles Freer to Stanford White, February 7, 1900, The New-York Historical Society.

250. *Northwest view, ca. 1912*

*251. Front, south view*

James L. Breese House
"The Orchard"
155 Hill Street
Southampton, New York
ca. 1898–1907

A writer for *House & Garden* magazine in 1903 conveyed a lasting image of the Breese house in Southampton: "One might not have been surprised to have suddenly looked in upon it through some old Virginia hedge, but upon the wind-swept Long Island shore, its impression becomes doubly vivid. . . . Everything is green and white: an American country house with almost tropically luxuriant vegetation all around it."[1] The southern Colonial image and particularly the Mount Vernon portico were used by the firm in several large country houses located in New England. Evidently for McKim, Mead & White, and their clients as well, the southern image seemed appropriate for the type of life they were attempting to convey—slow moving, leisurely and patrician. For them, it was one of the true American country-house idioms, comparable to the English country house.

In the Breese house the slender box posts of Mount Vernon were translated into thin Doric columns. This first impression is somewhat altered when the rear, or northern elevation and the interior staircase are viewed, for they appear to be more remindful of New England Federal architecture. Embedded within this semantic play of geographical references is the actual core of the house,

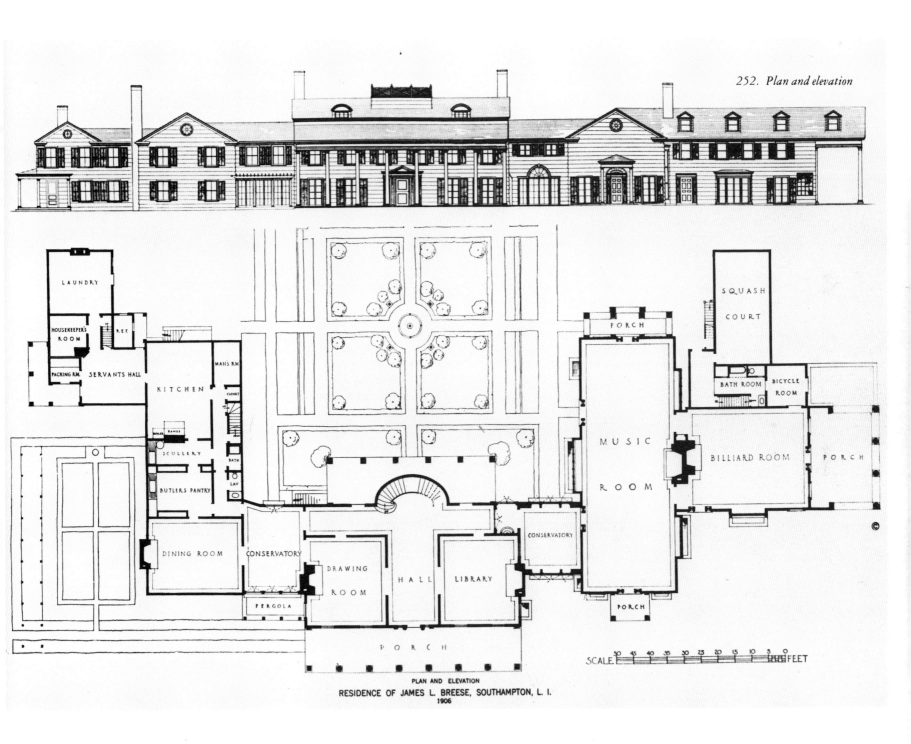

PLAN AND ELEVATION
RESIDENCE OF JAMES L. BREESE, SOUTHAMPTON, L. I.
1906

SCALE [50 45 40 35 30 25 20 15 10 5 0] FEET

LAUNDRY

HOUSEKEEPER'S ROOM

REF.

PACKING R.M.

SERVANTS HALL

KITCHEN

MANS RM.

CLOSET

BATH

LAV.

BOILER

RANGE

SCULLERY

BUTLERS PANTRY

DINING ROOM

CONSERVATORY

PERGOLA

DRAWING ROOM

HALL

LIBRARY

CONSERVATORY

PORCH

MUSIC ROOM

PORCH

BILLIARD ROOM

PORCH

SQUASH COURT

BATH ROOM

BICYCLE ROOM

PORCH

253. *Site plan*

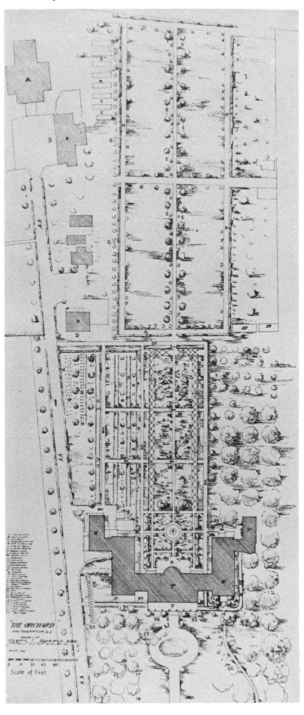

a Long Island farmhouse dating from the eighteenth century that was moved to the site. The exterior covering, hand-rived cypress shingles, wide and deep (a fourteen-inch square of each is left exposed) and painted white, makes reference to this Long Island Colonial origin.

James L. Breese, a New York financier, was a close social friend of McKim and White and both the partners had a hand in the design. Apparently McKim controlled the exterior, added the portico, and began the service wing extensions of the house incorporating some outbuildings.[2] White worked on the interiors, especially a remodeling of the music room in 1906–07. The overall order of the grounds and emphatic axiality of the garden may have been owed to McKim; however, White was responsible for many of the garden details. He commissioned a garden fountain from Janet Scudder, and in his own garden at St. James, White used herms very similar to those at "The Orchard."[3] Also assisting on the design were two employees of the firm, Frederick J. Adams and Harrie T. Lindeberg.[4] On the interior, the partners retained the original features of the older portion of the house. New fireplaces and the staircase added an air of refinement and elegance not originally present. The major focus of their work was the music room which measured seventy feet by twenty-eight feet and was eighteen feet high. Covered in a linenfold paneling, the room originally contained an extraordinary collection of White's European ravagings.

The formal garden was defined by brick herringbone-pattern walks and a Doric

254. *Music room*

James L. Breese House

pergola. Broken into different sections, such as rose garden and different types of flower beds, the garden in full bloom presented an extraordinary picture on the windswept, flat, Southampton landscape. A *House & Garden* writer summed up Southampton as "more fitting for endless rows of vanishing cabbages than the retreats and hidden shady nooks and walks of the ideal pleasure garden."[5] McKim, Mead & White succeeded in creating a rather evocative assemblage of images and spaces which indicated the range of sources they saw as appropriate for Americans.

In the late 1970s, after years of standing empty, the house and grounds were purchased by Sean W. Sculley of Simon Thoresen & Associates of New York, restored and sold as condominiums.

[1] John A. Gade, "Long Island Country Places, Designed by McKim, Mead & White II—'The Orchard' at Southampton," *House & Garden* III (March, 1903): 117.

[2] Charles Baldwin, *Stanford White* (New York: Dodd, Mead & Co., 1931), 326 assigns the house to White. Letter, Frances Breese Miller (Breese's daughter) to Author, October 5, 1973, remembers McKim being largely in charge. Materials at The New-York Historical Society and the Library of Congress indicate both partners had a hand.

[3] Janet Scudder, *Modeling my Life*, reprinted in Baldwin, *White*, 283.

[4] Letter, McKim to Breese, January 7, 1903, Library of Congress; and drawings for studio addition in possession of Robert White, Smithtown, N.Y.

[5] Gade, "Long Island Country Places": 126.

256. *Garden view to the north, 1980*

257. *Garden view to the south, ca. 1910*

201

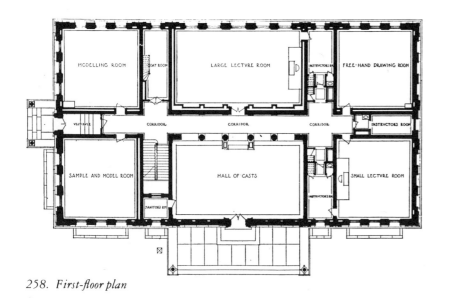

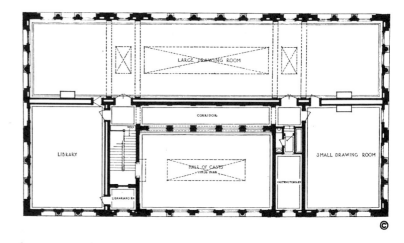

*258. First-floor plan*

*259. Second-floor plan*

*260. Front, south view*

## Robinson Hall, School of Architecture
Harvard University
Cambridge, Massachusetts
1899–1902

Most of the work the firm did for Harvard University can be ascribed to Charles McKim. While he never graduated, his attendance made him an alumni and, from 1889 onwards he was constantly involved with projects for rationalizing the sprawling campus. His first work was for a series of gates in commemoration of the different classes. In time he designed sixteen gates and the connecting fence that gave some sense of definition to the randomly built campus. Other plans concerned connecting the Yard with the Charles River. Hence when in 1899 the parents of Nelson Robinson, Jr., class of 1900, announced they would give $100,000 towards a new architecture building in memory of their son, McKim, Mead & White were the obvious choice. Not even a token competition was held.[1] H. Langford Warren, the head of the architecture school, worked closely with McKim throughout late 1899 and early 1900 in developing the plans.

Sited perpendicularly to H. H. Richardson's Sever Hall (1878) McKim's building carried on the Harvard Yard tradition of freestanding buildings creating spatial enclosures. It also was within the Harvard tradition of using red brick with light-colored trim. However, stylistically, it was not Georgian, nor Romanesque, but peculiarly American, Beaux-Arts

*261. Front detail*

classical. The building was encrusted with fragments that recall the Assyrian, Greek, Roman and Italian Renaissance ancestry of architecture. McKim took the fragments of antiquity that littered the entrance courtyard at the Ecole des Beaux-Arts in Paris and placed them on the wall of Robinson Hall. Names of great architectural figures from the past were placed in panels beneath the upper-floor windows. The plan was straightfor-

ward, with a large hall that served as the plaster-casts gallery at the front. The remainder of the interior was basically large uninterrupted spaces that could be used for a variety of purposes.

Robinson Hall was converted to general classroom use in the early 1970s when the architects left to take up residence in new modern quarters.

[1] Letter, President Charles Eliot to McKim, July 29, 1899, The New-York Historical Society.

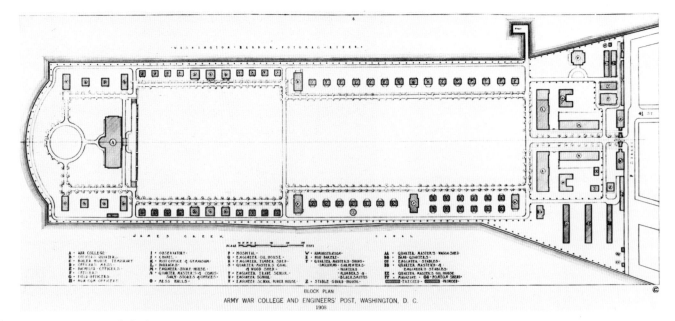

BLOCK PLAN
ARMY WAR COLLEGE AND ENGINEERS' POST, WASHINGTON, D. C.
1908

262. *Block plan, 1908*

263. *Early sketch by McKim, ca. 1902*

264. Aerial view, ca. 1970

Army War College
Fort Lesley J. McNair
Washington, D.C.
1902–08

The Army War College (now the National War College) is an impressive ensemble illustrative of McKim, Mead & White's large-scale planning abilities and their sense for dramatic ritual. The commission was a result of McKim's involvement in the Washington, D.C., Plan. During a lunch in January 1902, the plans for a new war college—intended to train senior staff in large-scale operations—were discussed by the colonel-in-charge for site at Fort McNair. After listening to the colonel's proposal, McKim responded:

*Now, Colonel Black, the trouble with you is that you have the heel of your stocking where the toe ought to be. In order to get the main building and the officer's quarters nearest town, you have put them facing the car-barns; and then you have located the barracks on the commanding point of land looking off towards Mount Vernon, down the broad Potomac pathway—more spacious than the Thames at London, the Seine at Paris, the Tiber at Rome, or the Danube at Vienna. The two locations should be reversed. Then, too, the houses for the officers should be along the river. Have regard to the climate and build them with broad piazzas, with white columns. Then you will have a regiment on parade!*[1]

The site at Fort McNair contained a ragged group of non-descript buildings. A peninsula into the Potomac and

265. *War College*

266. *Enlisted mens' barracks*

bounded by the Anacostia River and Washington Canal, it was nearly a fifth of a mile wide, and three quarters of a mile deep. McKim's arrangement called for a monumental gate, plain brick utilitarian service buildings and barracks to be placed near the entrance, which formed a forecourt and defined the axis of the peninsula. Opening from this would be a long parade field, defined on the sides by an enfilade of trees and officers' quarters. At the end, over a half-mile distant and facing north on the sea of green grass, would be the main building, a burly Beaux-Arts machine. Most of the important elements of McKim's scheme were carried out; the officers' quarters, large semi-Georgian houses of dark red brick and white trim and the plain brick barracks were built. The Army modified his designs for non-commissioned officers' quarters, removing the dormers and porticos, and some of the earlier buildings were never removed from the parade field. The gate was never built.

The main building is constructed entirely of brick and has Guastavino vaulting throughout. On the north it is fronted by a broad granite terrace-platform which, although never completed, was suitable for parade reviews and as a pedestal for statues of famous military leaders. Essentially a tough and austere structure, the major interior arrangements can be easily understood from the exterior. Two three-story-tall spaces—the map room and library—on either side of the domed entrance hall emerge as vaults at both ends. Natural light comes through the thermal clerestory

267. *War College*

268. *Officers' housing*

269. *Rotunda*

270. *Rotunda detail*

271. *War College. Pier base detail at entrance.*

272. *Library*

windows and end glazing. Arranged on either side of these major spaces are smaller office wings, which are carried on brick piers. Directly on the entrance axis is the auditorium which emerges at the rear (south) as an aspidal extrusion. Ionic columns in antis, and eagles mark the entrance and the vaulted ends. The entire brick structure is bounded and girded by thick, light-colored granite entablatures and moldings. The interior is relatively simple, though of great spatial drama, with the intersections of the ramps, vaults, galleries, lunettes and piers. The interplay of these forms, the vertical spatial movement, and the cascades of light recalls Piranesian interiors.

McKim's entire War College complex still exists in good condition, and recently the main building underwent some restoration.

[1]  Charles Moore, *The Life and Times of Charles Follen McKim* (Boston and New York: Houghton Mifflin Co., 1929), 201–02. See also, *Ceremonies at the Laying of the Cornerstone of the Army War College Building at Washington Barracks*, (Washington, D.C.: Government Printing Office, 1903); and *Fort Lesley J. McNair: A Brief History of the Post* (Washington, D.C.: The National War College, 1950).

273. *Main Waiting Room. View to north and Thirty-third Street entrance. Jules Guerin's murals are faintly visible.*

## The Pennsylvania Railroad Station
## New York, New York
## 1902–11
## Demolished

The intention behind Pennsylvania Station was straightforward—to create a monumental gateway to New York City, and to snare passengers and traffic from the competing New York Central Railroad that was concurrently erecting Grand Central Terminal across town. For years the Pennsylvania Railroad Company had been prevented from entering Manhattan by the Hudson River, too broad and too deep to bridge over or tunnel under. However, advances in tunnel construction and electrification (to replace steam locomotion) made entry into Manhattan more than a dream. The aggressive President, Alexander J. Cassatt, saw the new possibilities and commissioned Charles McKim in April 1902 to begin drawing up plans. Simultaneously, Cassatt had Daniel Burnham design Union Station in Washington, D.C. Cassatt wanted Pennsylvania Station to be both a successful business enterprise and also embody civic ideals. Initially he envisioned a station with a tall-skyscraper hotel attached, much in the manner of English and Continental rail stations. However, McKim was unalterably opposed to high-rise buildings on the grounds that they were anti-urban, and ultimately he prevailed and Cassatt agreed to drop the hotel. The result was one of McKim's most monumental and moving designs, a giant of a building that still retained a human scale. In catching

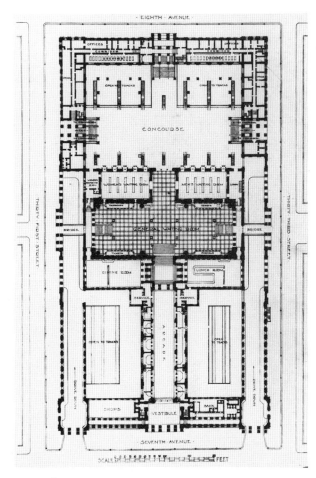

274. *Plan*

211

or meeting a train at Pennsylvania Station one became part of a pageant—actions and movements gained significance while processing through such grand spaces. Or as McKim's biographer said: "One does not rush to catch a Pennsylvania train—one proceeds to it in orderly but expeditious manner. It is only when looking down into the great waiting room from the head of one of the four staircases that one realizes that he is gazing into a space as large as the nave of St. Peter's, the biggest in Christendom."[1]

   The site of the building occupied two city blocks, between Seventh and Eighth Avenues and Thirty-first and Thirty-third Streets, or approximately eight acres. Below ground and out of site was another twenty-five acres of tracks that fanned throughout the area. The station was designed to handle both originating and terminating passengers for both local and long distance trains, to provide connections to the Long Island Railroad and to the Seventh and Eighth Avenue subways. McKim's problem was to create an orderly system that would bring passengers and baggage together. With the use of electric locomotives, tracks could be suppressed, and they were ultimately laid at forty-five feet below grade. McKim and his chief office associates, William Symmes Richardson and Tenunis J. Van Der Bent, worked out a series of paths by which pedestrians (both long distance and commuters) and vehicles had access to the station and yet were separate. Typically, the pedestrian had the more direct access; baggage was trucked to one end of the station, where underneath

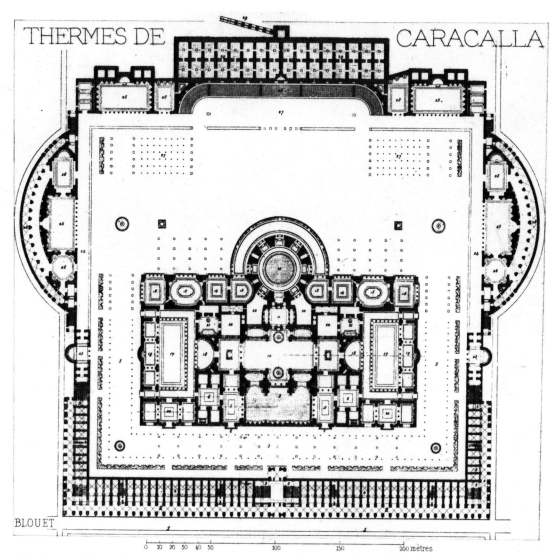

277. *Baths of Caracalla*

baggage cars could be located.

   The main public areas of the station received the most attention. For the general waiting room McKim drew upon the tepidarium of the Baths of Caracalla in Rome that he knew well from books such as D'Espouy and from first-hand

215

278. *Concourse. View of Thirty-third Street entrance.*

observation. In 1901, while with the McMillan Commission in Rome, he had photographs made of the baths with human figures positioned for scale.[2] The dimensions of the Roman baths were 80 feet by 175 feet and 110 feet high. McKim enlarged this to 108 feet by 280 feet and a height of 150 feet. Three massive groin vaults (in reality plaster shells) were supported by eight giant Corinthian columns. Murals by Jules Guerin portrayed the far-flung empire of the Pennsylvania Railroad and the American sphere of influence. Travertine marble covered the lower walls. Posed next to the grand waiting room, McKim situated the steel and glass concourse shell, 208 feet by 315 feet, that was similarly divided into three groin vaults. Between the two spaces, one of modern materials, the other of (seemingly) ancient prototypes, McKim obviously intended for a dialogue to take place on the nature of American civilization. From the concourse one proceeded down to the trains. The building also contained dining rooms, waiting rooms (segregated by sexes), office facilities, shops and a bank.

The Seventh Avenue facade was conceived of as the main facade and only it contained a full colonnade. The remaining facades all had similar large high attic entrance pavilions, and the walls were articulated by pilasters. Access to the station was from a variety of points, with one major entrance. A Tuscan Doric order was used on the exterior, and pink Milford granite was used as a sheathing material. Modulations in the wall plane, either through voids created by the columns, or more subtle projections and indentations, gave variety to the tremendously long enclosures. Adolph A. Weinman provided the architectural sculpture. From a distance, one could see the huge waiting room with its thermal windows projected up and beyond, and only partially visible was the lower and more modern steel and glass concourse. The entire building, while large and posturing, contained the air of an efficient machine, finely tuned and intended both to accommodate and to impress.

McKim worked steadily on the designs from April 1902 to 1904 when the first tunnel work began. In 1905 construction began on the building with the plans still somewhat incomplete. McKim's deteriorating health forced him to retire in 1906, and the project was largely completed by Richardson and Van Der Bent. He died in September 1909; the station was formally dedicated on August 1, 1910. Trains began to use it later that year, and in October 1911 the station was fully complete, about nine and a half years after the project was first broached.

By the 1950s the priorities of the Pennsylvania Railroad Company had changed, and they allowed the building to be brutally mutilated and to deteriorate. In 1963, after some ineffective protest, Pennsylvania Station was demolished. McKim's vision and that of Cassatt, seem to have been lost somewhere along the way.

[1]  Charles Moore, *The Life and Times of Charles Follen McKim* (Boston and New York: Houghton Mifflin & Co., 1929), 275–76. See also Westinghouse, Church, Kerr & Company, *The New York Passenger Terminal of the Pennsylvania Railroad* (New York, 1908).

[2]  Moore, *McKim*, 275

279. *Preliminary design in watercolor, ink and pencil on paper*

280. *Accepted design rendered in watercolor, ink and pencil on paper*

In April 1902, an obviously elated Charles McKim wrote to William Mead while on vacation in Europe:
*I will only preface by saying, that the country is safe, and I think you will agree, the office prospering, when I tell you of several new jobs in hand, as well as in prospect. Amongst these are J. Pierpont Morgan's, who telephoned my house a night or two ago, and the next morning at his house, informed me that he had purchased all the property between his house and Park Avenue on the north side of 36th Street, to be laid out architecturally and turned into a garden. . . . He proposes to cut off 28 feet at the eastern end for a house for his daughter, Louisa (who married Saterlee) and in the interval between the two build a little Museum building to house his books and collections.*[1]

The result, the Morgan Library which cost in excess of $1.2 million, is one of the firm's finest buildings. While McKim was very much the designer of the structure and poured his heart into the details, as a later partner observed, the delicacy of the structure is not typical of him at all. Rather McKim became known for his "great, simple, monumental buildings," and the Morgan Library was more typical of "his right hand," William Mitchell Kendall.[2]

John Pierpont Morgan controlled not only American and international finance

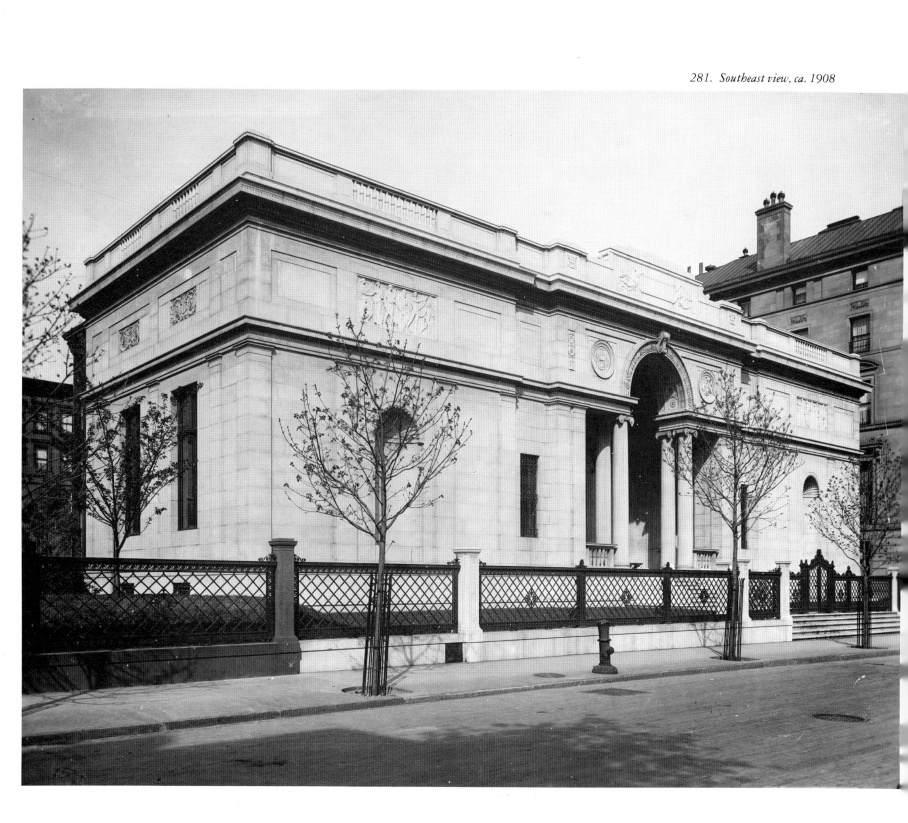

281. *Southeast view, ca. 1908*

*282. Entrance to Villa Medici, Rome*

*283. Entrance, 1908*

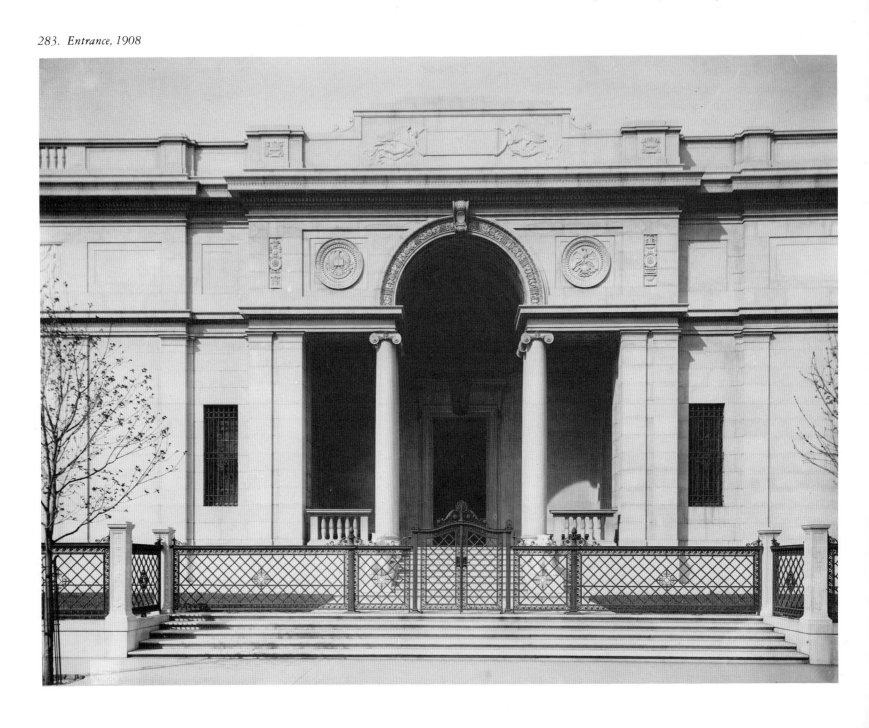

at the turn of the century, but also the international art market. An omnivorous collector, his passions ran in all directions, paintings, books and art objects. He had been known to purchase entire collections sight unseen. The library was intended as a repository for his finest books, paintings and art objects and as a private office. He continued to live next door in a brownstone.[3]

As early as 1900 Morgan had discussed the building with McKim and also with Whitney Warren, who had done some preliminary studies. After the meeting with Morgan in April 1902, McKim produced two designs: the first derived from Palladian villas, and the second, while having its origins certainly in Italian Renaissance garden casinos, was more suitable for an urban strongbox. With modifications, the second scheme became the accepted design. The closest source in McKim's own work was the Walker Art Gallery at Bowdoin College. The entrance loggia displayed McKim's (and Kendall's) scientific eclecticism, and was based upon a number of models such as the garden loggia at the Villa Giulia and the entrance at the Villa Medici in Rome. White marble was used as the building material. McKim envisioned a precision in the marble work similar to that of the ancient Greeks, and he related to Morgan his unsuccessful attempt to put a knife blade between the blocks of the Erectheum in Athens.[4] When Morgan expressed interest, even when learning that such precision would cost an extra $50,000, McKim ordered a "squeeze"—plaster cast—of the Erectheum from Gorham Stevens, a former

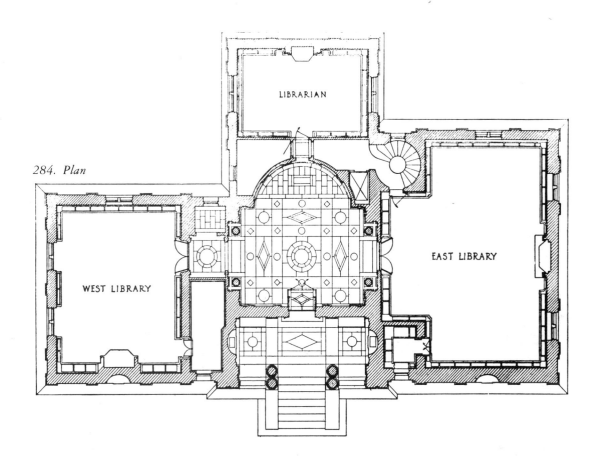

284. *Plan*

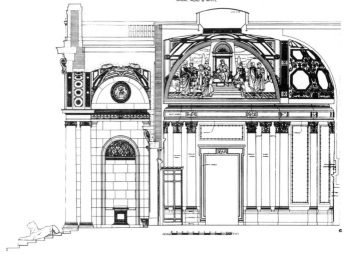

285. *Transverse section*

*286. Rotunda, 1956*

employee and then head of the American School of Classical Studies in Athens.[5]

The exterior exhibits McKim's characteristic restraint with ornament, with the major concentration at the entry. Andrew O'Conner provided the exterior relief sculpture. Twin frieze panels over the side niches portray *Tragic* and *Lyric Poetry*. McKim's head appears on a sphinx in the former panel. Library and printer's devices appear as other elements of the decoration. The twin lionesses on the steps were sculptured by Edward Clark Potter.

As the building was originally completed, Morgan occupied the west room as his study, and the east room was given over to books and displays. Interior decoration was a critical issue and McKim paid special attention to the symbolic implications of the different motifs used. The rotunda and east library were largely decorated by H. Siddons Mowbray, who had previously done work for McKim on buildings such as the University Club's library. McKim had paid for Mowbray's residence in Rome in 1902 to study first-hand examples of Italian Renaissance mural painting. In June 1904, Mowbray wrote to McKim that he intended "to go to Rome in September to make a careful study of the Villa Madama—before attempting the treatment."[6] The rotunda follows closely the style of the interior of the Villa Madama. Above the rich and colorful marble floor (following the pattern of the Villa Pia in the Vatican), walls and columns, Mowbray provided the usual muses, gods and figures of classical literature—from Homer to Sir Launcelot.

287. *East Room, 1956*

The east room's decoration is more restrained. Here Mowbray followed the style of Pinturicchio, especially in the Church of Santa Maria del Popolo, and arranged in the lunettes the disciplines—*Science, Architecture, Music*—and the famous figures—*Dante, Columbus, Caxton,* etc. Some of the figures such as *Music* were rendered in a nearly Art Nouveau manner. Below are the books, great Flemish tapestries and an ornate fireplace imported from Italy. The west room—Morgan's room—is in a sense more restrained and yet richer. Red damask silk printed with the Chigi arms covers the walls. On it are hung Morgan's favorite

223

288. *West Room, Morgan's office, 1956*

paintings by Cranach, Memling and others. The ceiling is of wood and deeply coffered. Reputedly from an Italian cardinal's palace, McKim actually purchased it from a Florentine antique dealer, and then hired James Wall Finn to paint decorations derived from antique bookplates and arms devices of cardinals and convents. So expertly did Finn replicate the antique that for years it has been interpreted as an original.[7]

In spite of the inevitable difficulties between the imperious Morgan and the stubborn McKim, a real affection and respect was evident in their relationship and the final building. Morgan became one of the prime supporters of McKim's American Academy in Rome. Near the completion of the building McKim could write to Stanford White: "Morgan, . . . most satisfied and gratified. . . . The sky is blue here and there is no occasion for worry."[8]

The library exists today in excellent condition and is open to the public.

[1]  Letter, McKim to Mead, April 2, 1902, Library of Congress.

[2]  Letter, Bert Fenner to R. Clipston Sturgis, January 10, 1924, The New-York Historical Society.

[3]  There have been several studies of Morgan, the best are: Cass Canfield, *The Incredible Pierpont Morgan* (New York: Harper & Row, 1974); Frederick Lewis Allen, *The Great Pierpont Morgan* (New York: Harper & Bros., 1949) and Calvin Tomlins, *Merchants and Masterpieces: The Story of the Metropolitan* (New York; E. P. Dutton, 1970).

[4]  Charles Moore, *The Life and Times of Charles Follen McKim* (Boston and New York: Houghton Mifflin & Co., 1929) ch. XXII, relates many details on the design and building.

[5]  Letter, McKim to Stevens, December 14, 1903, Library of Congress.

[6]  Letter, Mowbray to McKim, June 4, 1904, The New-York Historical Society. I am indebted to William Voelke, curator at the Morgan Library, for information on the building, and especially for his research into the interior decoration. Mr. Voelke mounted an exhibit on the building's design from December 1981 to January 1982.

[7]  Information from Mr. Voelke. See, Wayne Andrews, *Mr. Morgan and His Architect* (New York: The Pierpont Morgan Library, 1957), 9. Also, letters, McKim to Galleria Simontte, Rome and Signore Stefano Bardini, Florence, May 30, 1904, The New-York Historical Society, advising them he is looking for antique marble mantel pieces and a paneled ceiling.

[8]  Letter, McKim to White, February 1, 1906, The New-York Historical Society.

*Appendices*

# Bibliography

The literature and source material available on McKim, Mead & White is simply overwhelming, and no attempt is made here to create a comprehensive bibliography, which of necessity would be very long. Instead, I am merely listing the major depositories of original source material, and a brief listing of the essential literature on the firm.

*Original source materials:* The most comprehensive collection of material is at The New-York Historical Society where original drawings, blueprints, office correspondence and some personal correspondence has been placed. The Avery Architectural Library at Columbia University has a much smaller collection of materials relating to the firm, and recently, they have received from the White family considerable materials relating to Stanford White. The Museum of the City of New York has the firm's original glass-plate negatives of the New York City work. The Library of Congress has the personal and office correspondence of Charles McKim along with the papers of his biographer, Charles Moore. A minor collection of McKim's letters is at The New York Public Library. Many of the individual buildings designed by the firm have substantial collections relating to that particular project, i.e.: Harvard University, the Boston Public Library and individual house owners. It should be noted that materials relating to the early history of the firm, before 1890, are scarce.

*Basic literature includes:*

Baldwin, Charles. *Stanford White.* New York: Dodd, Mead & Co., 1939. Reprint. New York: Da Cappo Press, 1971.

Desmond, Henry W. and Croly, Herbert. "The Work of Messrs. McKim, Mead & White." *Architectural Record,* Vol. 20 (September 1906): 153–246.

Granger, Alfred Hoyt. *Charles Follen McKim: A Study of His Life and Work.* Boston and New York: Houghton Mifflin Co., 1913.

*A Monograph of the Works of McKim, Mead & White, 1879–1915.* 4 vols. New York: The Architectural Book Publishing Company, 1915–1920. Reprinted in one volume. New York: Benjamin Blom, 1973.

*A Monograph of the Works of McKim, Mead & White, 1879–1915. Students' Edition.* 2 vols. New York: The Architectural Book Publishing Company, 1925. Reprinted in one volume. New York: The Architectural Book Publishing Company, 1981.

Moore, Charles. *The Life and Times of Charles Follen McKim.* New York and Boston: Houghton Mifflin Co., 1929. Reprint. New York: Da Cappo Press, 1970.

Reilly, Charles. *McKim, Mead & White.* London: Ernest Benn, Ltd., 1924.

Roth, Leland. *The Architecture of McKim, Mead & White, 1870–1920: A Building List.* New York: The Garland Press, 1978.

———. "The Urban Architecture of McKim, Mead & White." Ph.D. diss., Yale University, 1973.

Sturgis, Russell. "The Work of McKim, Mead & White." *Architectural Record.* Great American Architects Series (May 1895).

Swarthwout, Egerton. "An Architectural Decade." Unpublished manuscript in offices of Cain, Ferril & Bell, New York, N.Y.

White, Lawrence Grant. *Sketches and Designs by Stanford White.* New York: The Architectural Book Publishing Company, 1920.

Wilson, Richard Guy; Pilgrim, Dianne; and Murray, Richard. *The American Renaissance 1876–1917.* Brooklyn and New York: The Brooklyn Museum and Pantheon Press, 1979.

Wilson, Richard Guy. "Charles F. McKim and the Development of the American Renaissance: A Study in Architecture and Culture." Ph.D. diss., University of Michigan, 1972.

——. "The Early Work of Charles F. McKim: Country House Commission." *Winterthur Portfolio* 14 (Autumn 1979): 235–67.

# Sources

1. Reprinted from Lawrence Grant White, *Sketches and Designs of Stanford White, 1920*

2. *Library of Congress, photo by Irving Underhill*

3. Reprinted from *American Architect and Building News, 1879*

4. Richard Guy Wilson

5. Robert White

6. Saint-Gaudens National Historical Site

7. Countesy of the Museum of the City of New York

8. Reprinted from the *Engineering Record, 1891*

9. Reprinted from *Monograph of the Works of McKim, Mead & White, 1915–1920*

10. Janet Davis

11. Richard Guy Wilson

12. Richard Guy Wilson

13. Richard Guy Wilson

14. Richard Guy Wilson

15. Richard Guy Wilson

16. Richard Guy Wilson

17. Reprinted from E. A. Morely, *Lenox, 1886*

18. Reprinted from George William Sheldon, *Artistic Country-Seats, 1886*

19. *Monograph of the Works of McKim, Mead & White, 1915–1920*

20. Richard Guy Wilson

21. *Monograph of the Works of McKim, Mead & White, 1915–1920*

22. Richard Guy Wilson

23. *Monograph of the Works of McKim, Mead & White, 1915–1920*

24. *Monograph of the Works of McKim, Mead & White, 1915–1920*

25. *Monograph of the Works of McKim, Mead & White, 1915–1920*

26. Courtesy of Roslyn Library, Long Island

27. Richard Guy Wilson

28. *American Architect and Building News, 1888*

29. Library of Congress, Detroit Photographic & Publishing Co

30. U.S. Commission of Fine Arts, Washington, D.C.

31. U.S. Commission of Fine Arts, Washington, D.C.

32. U.S. Commission of Fine Arts, Washington, D.C.

33. Richard Guy Wilson

34. Library of Congress, Detroit Photographic & Publishing Co

35. Library of Congress, Detroit Photographic & Publishing Co

36. Richard Guy Wilson

37. Richard Guy Wilson

38. Courtesy of Leland M. Roth

39. Richard Guy Wilson

40. Richard Guy Wilson

41. Richard Guy Wilson

42. Richard Guy Wilson

43. Art Commission of the City of New York

44. Library of Congress, Detroit Photographic & Publishing Co

45. *Monograph of the Works of McKim, Mead & White, 1915–1920*

46. Reprinted from D'Espouy, *Fragments d'Architecture du Moyen Age et de la Renaissance, 1897*

47. *New York Sketch Book of Architecture, 1874*

48. *Monograph of the Works of McKim, Mead & White, 1915–1920*

49. Richard Guy Wilson

50. Richard Guy Wilson

51. *Revue Generale de l'Architecture, 1853*

52. Library of Congress, photo by Irving Underhill

53. Reprinted from D'Espouy, *Fragments d'Architecture du Moyen Age et de la Renaissance, 1897*

54. *Monograph of the Works of McKim, Mead & White, 1915–1920*

55. Richard Guy Wilson

56. Richard Guy Wilson

57. U.S. Commission of Fine Arts, Washington, D.C.

58. Richard Guy Wilson

59. Reprinted from Claude Sauvageot, *Palais, Chateâux, Hotels et Maisons du France du XVᵉ au XVIIIᵉ Siècles, 1867*

60. Reprinted from Ferree, *American Estates and Gardens, 1904*

61. Reprinted from Claude Sauvageot, *Palais, Chateâux, Hotels et Maisons du France du XVᵉ au XVIIIᵉ Siècles, 1867*

148. Richard Guy Wilson

149. Richard Guy Wilson

150. Library of Congress, Historic American Building Survey, Cervin Robinson

151. Richard Guy Wilson

152. Richard Guy Wilson

153. Library of Congress, Historic American Building Survey, Cervin Robinson

154. Library of Congress, Historic American Building Survey, Cervin Robinson

155. Library of Congress, Historic American Building Survey, Cervin Robinson

156. Library of Congress, Historic American Building Survey, Cervin Robinson

158. Library of Congress, Historic American Building Survey, Cervin Robinson

159. Courtesy of Texas Historical Commission

160. Texas Historical Commission

161. Texas Historical Commission

162. Reproduced with the permission of the Rosenberg Library, Texas

163. Drexel Turner

164. Private collection

165. Private collection

166. Private collection

167. Emily Hoxie

168. Emily Hoxie

169. Emily Hoxie

170. Emily Hoxie

171. Emily Hoxie

172. Private collection

173. Private collection

174. Private collection

175. *American Architect and Building News*, 1888

176. Library of Congress, Detroit Photographic & Publishing Co

177. Library of Congress, Detroit Photographic & Publishing Co

178. Richard Guy Wilson

179. Courtesy of the Trustees of the Boston Public Library

180. Richard Guy Wilson

181. Richard Cheek

182. *American Architect and Building News*, 1888

183. *Monograph of the Works of McKim, Mead & White*, 1915–1920

184. *American Architect and Building News*, 1888

185. *American Architect and Building News*, 1888

186. Paul-Marie Letarouilly, *Edifices de Rome Moderne*, 1840–1857

187. Library of Congress, Detroit Photographic & Publishing Co

188. *American Architect and Building News*, 1888

189. Trustees of the Boston Public Library

190. Richard Guy Wilson

191. Richard Guy Wilson

192. Library of Congress, Detroit Photographic & Publishing Co

193. Library of Congress, Detroit Photographic & Publishing Co

194. Richard Guy Wilson

195. Library of Congress, Detroit Photographic & Publishing Co

196. Library of Congress, Detroit Photographic & Publishing Co

197. Richard Guy Wilson

198. Richard Guy Wilson

199. Richard Guy Wilson

200. Richard Guy Wilson

201. Courtesy of The New-York Historical Society, New York City

202. Richard Guy Wilson

203. The New-York Historical Society, New York City

204. The New-York Historical Society, New York City

205. Richard Guy Wilson

206. Richard Guy Wilson

207. Richard Guy Wilson

208. Richard Guy Wilson

209. Richard Guy Wilson

210. Courtesy of Farleigh Dickinson College, New Jersey

211. Richard Guy Wilson

212. Richard Guy Wilson

213. Farleigh Dickinson College, New Jersey

214. Richard Guy Wilson

215. Courtesy of Bowdoin College, Maine

216. *Monograph of the Works of McKim, Mead & White*, 1915–1920

217. Bowdoin College, Maine

218. Courtesy of the Rhode Island Development Council

219. *Monograph of the Works of McKim, Mead & White*, 1915–1920

220. The New-York Historical Society, New York City

221. Photo by William Barrett

222. William Barrett

223. William Barrett

224. State of Rhode Island and Providence Plantations

225. The New-York Historical Society, New York City

226. *Monograph of the Works of McKim, Mead & White*, 1915–1920

227. Library of Congress, Detroit Photographic & Publishing Co

228. *Monograph of the Works of McKim, Mead & White*, 1915–1920

229. Library of Congress, Detroit Photographic & Publishing Co

230. Library of Congress, Detroit Photographic & Publishing Co

231. *Monograph of the Works of McKim, Mead & White*, 1915–1920

232. Courtesy of The Brooklyn Museum

233. The New-York Historical Society, New York City

234. The New-York Historical Society, New York City

235. The Brooklyn Museum

236. The Brooklyn Museum

237. Library of Congress, Detroit Photographic & Publishing Co

238. The Brooklyn Museum

239. Library of Congress

240. Library of Congress, Detroit Photographic & Publishing Co

241. *The University Club*, 1900

242. *The University Club*, 1900

243. *Monograph of the Works of McKim, Mead & White*, 1915–1920

244. *The University Club*, 1900

245. Courtesy of the University Club

246. Courtesy of the University Club, photo by Thomas Venditi

247. The New-York Historical Society, New York City

248. *Monograph of the Works of McKim, Mead & White*, 1915–1920

249. Courtesy of Silver's

250. Library of Congress, Detroit Photographic & Publishing Co

251. *Monograph of the Works of McKim, Mead & White*, 1915–1920

252. *Monograph of the Works of McKim, Mead & White*, 1915–1920

253. Reprinted from *House and Garden*, 1903

254. Courtesy of Frances Breese Miller

255. Frances Breese Miller

256. Courtesy of Simon Thoreson Associates, New York

257. Frances Breese Miller

258. *Monograph of the Works of McKim, Mead & White*, 1915–1920

259. *Monograph of the Works of McKim, Mead & White*, 1915–1920

260. Richard Guy Wilson

261. Richard Guy Wilson

262. *Monograph of the Works of McKim, Mead & White*, 1915–1920

263. Courtesy of National Defense University, Washington, D.C.

264. National Defense University, Washington, D.C.

265. Richard Guy Wilson

266. Richard Guy Wilson

267. Richard Guy Wilson

268. Richard Guy Wilson

269. National Defense University, Washington, D.C.

270. National Defense University, Washington, D.C.

271. Richard Guy Wilson

272. National Defense University, Washington, D.C.

273. Library of Congress, Irving Underhill

274. *Monograph of the Works of McKim, Mead & White*, 1915–1920

275. Library of Congress, Irving Underhill

276. Library of Congress, Irving Underhill

277. D'Espouy, *Fragments d'Architecture du Moyen Age et de la Renaissance*, 1897

278. Library of Congress, Irving Underhill

279. The New-York Historical Society, New York City

280. Courtesy of Pierpont Morgan Library

281. Library of Congress, Detroit Photographic & Publishing Co

282. D'Espouy, *Fragments d'Architecture du Moyen Age et de la Renaissance*, 1897

283. Library of Congress, Detroit Photographic & Publishing Co

284. *Monograph of the Works of McKim, Mead & White*, 1915–1920

285. *Monograph of the Works of McKim, Mead & White*, 1915–1920

286. Pierpont Morgan Library

287. Pierpont Morgan Library

288. Pierpont Morgan Library

# Index